Faith, Family and Friends

Also by

Janice B. Holland

Beacons, Prayers, and Processes: Pathways to Healing

Tapestry: Poetic Threads of Life – Work included in this
Anthology of Poems

Faith, Family and Friends

Janice B. Holland, et al

Trafford
PUBLISHING®

ISBN: 978-1-4251-5089-1 (sc)
ISBN: 978-1-4251-5090-7 (e)

Trafford rev. 03/18/2011

 www.trafford.com

North America & International
toll-free: 1 888 232 4444 (USA & Canada)
phone: 250 383 6864 ♦ fax: 812 355 4082

"I have been crucified with Christ; and it is no longer I who live, but Christ lives in me; and the life which I now live in the flesh I live by faith in the Son of God, who loved me and gave Himself up for me."

Galatians 2:20

Preface

To make this a true book about faith, family, and friends, I chose to ask my only child, Cindy, and several of my friends who are also writers in their own right, if they would allow me to use some of their works. I also selected some of my favorite passages from God's Word as He calls me friend and loves me unconditionally. My works are noted either with the initials jab (before marriage) or jbh (after marriage). The works of my daughter or my friends are clearly identified by their names. A short note about each of the authors is included at the end of the book.

I am indebted to each of the contributors not only by their additions to this book but also by how they have greatly influenced my life in such positive ways. I hope you will be just as blessed by each of the works included. Godspeed to each of you!

Twenty-five percent of the author's profits on every book sold will be donated to charity, including but not necessarily limited to church missions and H-E-A-R-T (Hope Exists After Rape Trauma) of Suffolk.

TABLE OF CONTENTS

Faith

Family

Friends

INTRODUCTION
<u>Sharing One's Faith</u>

In Hebrews 11:1, we read "Faith is the assurance of things hoped for, the conviction of things not seen."[1] Webster defines faith as "confidence, conviction in regard to religion; system of religious beliefs; strict adherence to duty and promises, word or honor pledged."[2] Thus, we have God's definition and man's definition of faith. How then do we merge the two to explain our individual faith to others? Is it something we need to do since it has already been done?

From my perspective, it is not so much the believer's responsibility to define what has already been defined as it is to share demonstrations of God's divine intervention and acts of faith performed by people in the face of incredible odds with a world full of cynics and unbelievers. This is essential so others will also have the opportunity to know the peace that surpasses all understanding that can only be found in an intimate, personal relationship with Christ Jesus, our Lord and Savior. Even believers go through periods of troubles and tribulations that sorely test their faith. Such was the case with my family and closest friends as a series of circumstances with the force of Hurricane Katrina, immediately followed by her sister, Rita, stormed through my family between 2000 – 2006.

Without going into detail of each, the highlights included but are not limited to: my only sibling was diagnosed with prostrate cancer; both my parents died within nineteen months of each other; my husband had a freak fall, causing fourteen facial fractures that almost took his life; and, I contracted a rare virus that almost took my life before it was properly diagnosed. Additionally, my husband lost two different jobs because the companies he worked for went bankrupt (the first causing serious financial problems for us); my only child developed a serious illness; and I was diagnosed with five chronic illnesses. Topping it off, I began having major problems at work; one of my best friends attempted suicide in my presence; and, I began dealing with post-traumatic stress from finally coming to grips with being sexually abused for over ten years as a child. To say that our individual and family faith was not sorely tested would make me the biggest liar any reader ever met. Yet, I can assure you it was our individual and our collective faith that safely brought us to where we now are. The rest of the story will explain how God worked in our lives to keep us from falling. I believe our story is but one of many examples of how God helps restore faith in tough times. We must learn to listen for Him in the silence and look for the many, many signs He sends us daily.

The week this was written, I was able to celebrate Christmas with my brother and his family. He is cancer free and has passed that all-important five year mark. Praise the Lord! There is so much more to his story, however. You see, he was diagnosed as part of a routine physical.

"What's so unusual about that?" I hear you thinking. The answer is if his doctor had received the correct lab work, I likely would no longer have a brother who could celebrate with me. His lab report was mixed up with someone else by the same name. As a result, he was required to have an emergency biopsy, which led to immediate surgery. It was that early diagnosis that saved him. Only after his surgery did we learn his lab report showed a false negative. At his age, he would not have had another test for several years, which likely would have been too late as he was not having any symptoms. Coincidence, or God's intervention? My faith says God's intervention.

A little over a year later, we learned my father had stage four lung cancer and had less than six months to live. As it turned out, he only lived six weeks from the day of his diagnosis. He spent his last twelve days in the hospital. My mother's health prevented her from spending nights with him so I decided to do that for her, knowing my brother and my father normally did not do well together for long periods of time. It soon became apparent to me that my father was not going to leave the hospital alive. Realizing my brother needed to make peace with our dad, I called him at work and told him I needed to return to work the next day, and asked him if he would sit with Pop. He said he would. Our father asked Jimmy to cook him some of his famous beer-batter bass filets for supper that afternoon. As it turned out, it was to be my dad's last meal. I arrived to relieve him shortly after they had eaten together—mom, dad, and son. As my brother prepared to take Mom home, my dad said, "Jimmy, that's the best fish I've ever had. You've been a good son."

Mom leaned over to kiss him goodbye for the evening. "See you tomorrow," she said through her tears, amazed at what he had just said.

"You'll see me but I won't see you," he replied. "I love you, Snookums," he added strongly, using his pet name for her. Everyone just grinned at him, puzzled at his statement, as he was having the best day since he had been in the hospital.

Around 10 p.m., I realized Pop had taken a turn for the worse. I slipped out of his room, called Jimmy, and asked him to return to the hospital. I also called my daughter, who was in the midst of mid-term exams, and told her to plan to come home immediately after she finished the next morning's test as I thought the end was near. She told me during the call she was struggling with her faith. I asked her to be strong and told her we would discuss it when she got home the next day.

At midnight, Pop instructed the respiratory therapist not to come back. When the RT looked at my brother and I for reassurance, we indicated Pop was still in his "right" mind and could make his own decisions. About 2 a.m., Pop asked us who the man was standing behind the head of his bed. Since the head of his bed was braced against the wall, it was physically impossible for anyone to be there which we told him. He looked back at that spot and a look of calm overtook him. He smiled at the person and just said, "Never mind. I know who it is."

Pop woke up several different times over the next couple of hours to tell us a few last things. At 6:30 a.m., he asked my brother to go home to get our mother. You had to know Pop to understand there was to be no argument about who was to get her and that it was to be done then. He dozed briefly, then looked up at me and said, "Where's your mother?"

I told him that Jimmy was not yet back with her. He smiled sweetly and said, "You know what? I'm looking at her, she's looking at me, and we're both smiling." It was 7:08 a.m. Then he told me he loved me, closed his eyes and went to sleep. I laid my head on his chest and waited as his heart slowly stopped beating. I knew he died happy as he had seen my mom for the last time and that was all that mattered to him. He died at 7:18 a.m.

As you have guessed, my brother did not get my mom to the hospital before my father died. I'm sure both my heavenly and earthly fathers knew my mom's heart would never take the strain of watching him die. I asked my brother if he knew what time Mom opened the door when he went to get her. He said, "Yes, it was 7:08." When I asked how he could be so sure, he told me Mom had asked him the time. I asked if she smiled when she saw him. He indicated she had smiled as sweetly as he had ever seen. God's intervention so a dying man could see his lovely wife of almost 58 years one last time? My family says absolutely.

Was it Christ standing behind my father's bed at 2 a.m.? I won't know until I join him again. I do know whomever he saw gave him great peace. I also know sharing that information with my daughter recharged the batteries of her faith. I've also had reason to witness instances of similar things when my mother and two great aunts died since that night. I am certain believers are personally escorted to the next realm either by Christ, Himself, or by an angel dubbed worthy by Him. This would be a person the believer would recognize and feel secure going with as it would mean entry into his/her heavenly home.

I was on my way home from having dinner with a close friend after a very intense session with my therapist this particular Tuesday night when I decided to check the voice mails on my cell phone. When I noted one from my good friend, Jill, (name changed for the purpose of this story) I smiled wondering what funny message she might have left me this time. She was not her usually peppy self as she described a bad day at work, closing with her normal wish I would sleep well and she hoped I had a better day than she. Next, she told me she hoped I knew how much I had meant to her all the years since we had met in college. I could feel all the hair on the back of my neck stand at attention. It wasn't so much what she said but the slight catch in her voice as she said it. Somehow, I knew she was telling me goodbye—that she planned to end her life that night. Not wanting to waste time by pulling off the road to check what time she called, I drove with one hand on the wheel while manipulating the phone with the other to determine how long it had been since she had left that message. God certainly protected me and everyone else on the road as I was doing that.

"*Thank God,*" I remember thinking. "*It's only been about 45 minutes since she called. Maybe I still have time to get to her.*"

Of course, getting to her in time meant if she was home. I had no idea where else to look if she wasn't. I happened to be only ten minutes from her house when I checked my messages, as her home is between my therapist's office and my home. I frantically began calling her both at her house and on her cell phone but to no avail. "Come on, Jill, answer the damn phone," I yelled repeatedly into the phone as if it would make a difference.

I came to a red light and had to stop. A small, still voice said, "Try prayer." I literally looked around to see who spoke to me. Of course, no one was there, but I knew who had spoken.

"Please, dear God. I don't know what's going on with my dear friend, Jill, but everything in me tells me she's in a bad way. Please let her be home when I get there and let her still be in some shape I can save her. There has to be a reason you let me receive this call tonight before I got across the bridge," I prayed fervently. A sense of calm settled over me and I knew at the very least I would find Jill at home and alive when I arrived.

Just a few minutes later, I pulled in front of her house. There she sat, stony-faced on her front porch. The hour-long conversation that took place is unimportant because she rebuffed everything I said to her. When I believed I had nothing left in my bag of tricks to share with her, her daughter arrived home.

"What's wrong, Mom?" she asked.

"Nothing," Jill replied.

The daughter looked askance of me. "Your mom is planning to take her life tonight," I said, hoping it would shock Jill into realizing she needed help.

"MOM, NO!" her daughter cried out.

"Yes, I have nothing left to live for," Jill replied with no emotion. Another twenty minutes of conversation with her daughter and I did nothing to change her mind. Finally, frustrated the two of us would not leave her alone, Jill quietly walked into her house, went straight into her bathroom, locked the door, and took a large quantity of pills.

I looked at her daughter and said, "Call 9-1-1!" When she hesitated, I gave her my best mean assistant superintendent's look and tersely exclaimed, "NOW!"

About that time, Jill came out of the bathroom and climbed into bed to die. She was stunned and angry when personnel from fire, rescue and the police department arrived shortly thereafter and took her to the hospital against her will after ascertaining that she had taken a large amount of medication that was going to do her in if immediate action was not taken. Trust me; friend was not the term she used as they wheeled her out her front door.

As I sat in the hospital at 2 a.m., talking to Jill's husband, daughter and son and waiting for word on how Jill was doing, I shared with them just how amazing it was I even happened to be in the area that night. Normally, I saw my therapist on Monday nights but she had called the previous week to ask me to change to Tuesday so she could attend a function in another city. As a rule, I could not have made the switch as my job required me to work almost every Tuesday night but this particular Tuesday's meeting had been canceled because the superintendent was going to be at a conference. Usually, my after therapy dinner with my other friend would have been over long before the call came in, but, as I alluded to earlier, it had been one of those intense sessions requiring a fair amount of examination afterwards. Jill's husband was convinced she only called me because she knew I normally had a meeting that night and the deed would be done before I could do anything about it. A lucky set of coincidences or God's intercessions? My faith tells me they were all God's intercessions because if just one of them had not worked, my friend would be dead instead of celebrating her 55th birthday this year.

These are three examples of how the awesome God we serve has worked in not only my life but in the lives of my family and friends. While I sometimes lose my way, it does not last for long because I know God is, has been, and always will be faithful. Psalm 31:23-24 states "...The Lord preserves the faithful. ... Be strong and let your heart take courage all you who hope in the Lord."[3]

My hope, my faith, my all is in the Lord. I pray you will find something in this book to help you find the same.

In Christian Love,

Janice B. Holland

[1] New Inductive Study Bible. Harvest House Publishers, Eugene, Oregon, 2000.
[2] Webster's Dictionary and Roget's Thesaurus. Paradise Press, Inc., Weston, Florida, 2005 Edition
[3] New Inductive Study Bible.

Values

If
we
don't
value
the
people
and
things
that
matter

Hearts will definitely shatter!

jbh
1-20-08

L-shaped poem was developed by *Emotional Soldier,* a Fanstory writer.

Faith

"Faith is the assurance of things hoped for, the
conviction of things not seen."

Hebrews 11:1

IS GOD DEAD?

Is God dead?
Listen to the birds
While they proclaim Him;
Look at the meadow
Filled with beauty;
Gaze at the sky
In the morning dawn,
In the golden sunset,
In beautiful array

Tell me, is God dead?
Behold the beauty
Of forests in the fall;
Witness the innocence
Of a newborn child;
Breathe a breath
Of fresh country air
Then tell me
God is dead.

No, God is not dead.
He dwells in life,
In the living.
How do I know?
I felt His presence
In the calm
That comes after a storm.
That's how I know
God is not dead.

jab
1968

Imagine This Life

Imagine, if you can,
What would be lower than
Being born in a manger

Imagine if you would
Just what else ever could
Place a baby in more danger

Could you please tell me this
Is there something amiss
When a twelve-year-old is left behind

Would you please set me straight
What would have been His fate
If God's light on Him didn't shine

Now what do you think
Those people would drink
If water hadn't been turned into wine

After all, that wasn't the day
He had planned to display
That He really was Divine

Now don't you just wish
Just once you could fish
With the Man from Galilee

Not one hook in a gill
Yet the net He did fill
With fish from an angry sea

I wonder what it'd be like
Just once to take a hike
With Holy God's only Son

Whose cross on Calvary
Saved a poor wretch like me
And now the battle is won

If I take time every day
To ask Him to go my way
From me, He never will part

Not only will we be able to walk
We'll have forever to talk
With Him right here in my heart

        jbh
       12-14-07

Faithful Living

Faithful
Heartfelt belief
Knowing without seeing
Father, Jesus, Holy Spirit
Living

Desirée Cote Bryant
January, 2008
6 years old

Easter, 2005

I feel the pain before opening my eyes
And wonder why I even bother to rise
Then I look onto a glorious morning
Remembering instantly this is Easter ~
Easter, the most wonderful morning of all
At once, I'm reminded my pain is negligible
As compared to the pain our Savior, Jesus
      Christ,
So willingly bore not only for my sins
But for the sins, past, present, and future
Of all who have, are, or will be part of this world.
It is then my heart messages my brain
Instead of wondering why I should get up
I have an obligation to not only arise
But to go forth to share His words and His deeds
Such that others will be drawn to Him,
Be touched by His unconditional, sacrificial love
So they might have eternal life once this one is done.

      jbh
      3-27-05

<u>No Matter Why We Come</u>

I sought refuge in the house of God
To escape the confusion in mine
More prevalent during weekends
Than any other time of week
Fortunately my greatest time of need
Often matched the "open" hours of church
Making it a perfect sanctuary
For one seeking answers and escape

Unlike today when the media sensationalizes
        everything
I didn't have an avenue to share my concerns then
Nor in any way did I dare show the depths of my pain
Instead I threw myself into all the church had to offer
Sunday School lessons, sermons, choirs, youth
        groups,
The more time required away from home the better
Never realizing God was carefully crafting the
        foundation
Which would ultimately support all aspects of my life

I was simply unable to hear, speak and sing words of
        faith
Several times a week, most weeks of the year
Without being touched by the Holy Spirit
All the while gaining strength in my weak areas
Receiving support from others garnered in God's
        name
My every need being prayed for
Even when those needs were scarcely known by me
But surely known by an all loving and merciful God

Thus it is with the God we serve
He cares not why any of us come to Him
Rather that we come and listen to His word

So each of us can decide
To invite Christ into our heart
For He will not come uninvited
Even though He paid the ultimate sacrifice
For the right to do exactly that

Allow me, I pray, to invite you into God's house
No matter your reason for coming
Trust He'll do for you
All He's done for me,
A sinner simply seeking answers and escape
Found a safe harbor and foundation
Built upon a solid rock of salvation—
Come on in—
He'll do the same for you

jbh
12-14-05

WHY DO WE WAIT?

Oh, Lord,
Why is it all too often we come to you
Only when everyone and everything we have is gone?
Do we not realize You are also with us
In normal times and times of prosperity
With a desire to rejoice with us?
Why don't we discuss our good times with You
Just as we choose to pour out our nothingness to You
In broken voices filled with tears?
Do we simply believe because You are God
You have no need to hear our praises of
       Thanksgiving
When our lives have been so richly blessed
With treasures beyond our wildest imaginations
Most often with more than we could ever need
As we take so much for granted
While barely giving You lip service
In terms of true gratitude?
Instead, when we begin losing our grip
We turn to things of this world
Rather than first relying on You,
Our one true wise God, our Father.
I wonder what it would ultimately take to teach us
To turn to You for everything
Every day
Whatever comes our way
Instead of waiting for You to become our everything
Only when our everything is gone?

     jbh
     12-14-05

WHAT ARE YOU DOING WITH ME?

Lord, what are you doing with me
Replacing impatience with peace,
Teaching me to use waiting moments
To reflect upon all Thy hands have made?

Father, when were the blinders removed
Covering my eyes as cataracts
Blinding me from the beauty
Surrounding every phase of life?

My God, how patiently You waited
For me to include You in everything;
The fullness of Your mercy and grace
A simple invitation away.

Oh, Father, how You love me
In spite of my wretchedness,
Your Son, Jesus, becoming sin
So that I can be wholly clean.

Lord, continue filling me,
Bending, shaping, and molding me
Until I become the person
You desire me to be.

jbh
3-23-06

Death Came

Death came
  with it came heartbreak,
Death came
  with it came loneliness.

Death came
  as a cat
    slowly stalking
        her innocent victim.

Death came
  softly
      silently
In the middle of the night

The phone rang –
I knew it was the end
Another life snuffed
  like a candle
      in the wind.

Death came
  was proud
      yet did not win

For though death came
Another life began
  a better life
    one of love
          contentment
A life with the Master.

            jab
          7-31-68

Sometimes God Sends A Child

The young child smiled in wonder
As he sat on his grandpa's knee
Looking forward to the festivities
In search of their Christmas tree.

Perched in his favorite position
The child wiggled with delight
It was just to be the two of them
On their special quest that night.

The grandpa cherished the moment
As contentment filled his heart
For the journey that brought them together
Had such a precarious start.

He thought back to his grandson's birth
Doctors said he might not live
But they couldn't see past that moment
To the joy this child would give.

They thought his life would be limited
Facing obstacles at every turn,
Fearing there'd be much he couldn't do
And much he wouldn't learn.

To this child each day was a wonder
For no two days were ever the same
He never saw the same thing twice,
And nothing was bland or mundane.

As the grandpa eyed the fraziers
The white pines and spruces, too,
He knew the child would know which tree
Would be the only one that would do

Though the grandfather saw the splendor
And the beauty in every one
He knew the boy had an eye for such
And their looking was not yet done

And then the child came to a stop
He couldn't believe his eyes
There stood the perfect tree
Making it the perfect prize

The boy fell in love with the tree
He saw potential where others saw none.
He perceived its hidden beauty,
And he knew this was the one.

The tree was kind of squatty,
Some limbs hung limp and low
But to the child it mattered not
For when planted it would grow.

The grandson carefully explained,
"The tree and I are both unique.
We might be small in stature
But we're more than our physique."

"Though we are the smallest of the lot
In the wind we still can dance.
We each have overcome obstacles
When others didn't give us a chance."

He knew he'd never run fast,
And sometimes he'd stumble and fall
He would never be the strongest
Nor in height would he grow tall.

He wouldn't often win trophies
There are sports he'd never play.
He was content to be able to explore
The wonders of each new day.

With pride the grandpa recognized
Through eyes misted with his tears,
That this little child's wisdom
Was well beyond his years.

He embraced each and every moment
Welcoming the sunshine of each day
Never passing judgment
On what others do or say.

The grandpa bowed his head in prayer
Sending thanks to God above
For giving him this blessing
This precious gift of love.

God doesn't always send angels
When there is a special need
Sometimes He sends a child instead,
To do an angel's deed.

        Marcia L. Gray
        Christmas, 2006

That Moment

That moment when
> twilight turns to night
> darkest night becomes dawn
> ebb tide comes and goes
How do we know ~

The instant when
> stranger becomes friend
> heartaches begin to mend
> no longer have to pretend
Then I know ~

The minute that
> I first believed
> fell down on my knees
> prayed for my release
Did it show ~

The very second He
> came to my side
> forever to abide
> joy I couldn't hide
Did you know ~

The exact hour when you
> invite Jesus to be
> the One who sets you free
> without uncertainty
You will glow ~

The moment you first know
     the Savior's purest love
     gentle as a dove
     sent from God above
For us to share ~

The first breath when you wake
     take some time to pray
     praise His name each day
     from Him never stray
So all others will know ~

The moment we came to Him
     was really when life began
     now following His plan
     so much better than
Living this life alone!

       jbh
       7-10-07

BETHLEHEM'S CHILDREN

Children gather at the altar
learning spiritual lessons
from faithful women
sharing God's promises
so they will be well-armed
for battling the enemy

Children's choirs sharing joy
through praise and worship
singing their need for Jesus
declaring they'll be sunbeams for Him
surrendering all and knowing also
He loves them above all

Our children are strong
growing in faith and service
willing to affirm who they are
by sharing with the congregation
and going into the community
making positive impacts on all they meet

Just don't understand the children today
is what I often hear too many say
then our youth they need to see
feeding the hungry, clothing the poor,
assisting the needy, and so much more,
adults should do as well, don't you agree?

        jbh
      7-22-07

Interlude on I-95

"M'am, I'm not going to hurt you," are not the words you want to hear when you are traveling alone and standing in front of a drink machine at a rest stop along an Interstate highway at night. One could even be forgiven for struggling when those words were immediately followed by, "I've never done anything like this before." Amazingly, I became intrigued by the woman who had selected me from those travelers who had chosen this spot as a respite from I95 just 40 miles north of the SC/NC border.

"How can I help you?" I inquired. She quickly gave me her name and told me haltingly she had been robbed and had no money for food or fuel to get home. I quickly glanced around to determine if the robber was still around.

"Where is your vehicle?" I asked, thinking maybe someone had stolen her car while she was inside the rest area. She pointed to her car which was parked nearby.

"When were you robbed?" I questioned as I was still trying to determine if we both may be at risk.

"About 13 hours ago," she said, "in Georgia."

I suppose my confusion was apparent so she gave me her name again and said the robber had taken her jewelry and purse. She had been able to travel this far with the money she had on her person and the fuel in her car. She had been in Georgia due to the death of her mother who had Alzheimer's and was living in a nursing home. She had to take care of everything because she was an only child. I asked if there was anyone I could call. She sadly shook her head no. She indicated that her husband was in Afghanistan and she had left messages for some other people who had not yet returned her calls.

I asked where she lived. She first wanted to know where I lived. When I said I was from Virginia, she burst into tears. When she could talk, she indicated she was from Roanoke. I told her my daughter had gone to school at Radford University (about 40 miles south of Roanoke) and her best friend lived in Roanoke. By now, the lady was crying profusely.

With searching eyes, she asked if I was a preacher or a teacher. As I was wearing a yellow Oxford shirt, green jeans, and tennis shoes, and no identification, there was nothing to identify me with any profession. However, I chose to answer her question and relayed I was a retired educator. She asked what I taught so I gave her a quick outline of my years as a teacher, assistant principal, principal and assistant superintendent even as I was trying to determine what this woman really needed from me. I was still struggling with the idea I was being set up to be robbed, or worse, as she talked.

She questioned where I was traveling from and where I was headed. I explained I had just spent three wonderful days at the East National Conference for Christian Counselors. She wondered how a retired educator would find herself there. I felt led to tell her I was molested and later raped by a friend of my father's and now felt called by God to become a "wounded healer." She reached out to touch me on the arm, in a gesture of comfort and sisterhood, and stated that she had been raped a year and a half ago. I expressed my regrets and asked if she was okay. With glistening eyes, she said she was and her rapist was in jail. I asked if she was getting any help. She said she had at one time but with her mom's situation had stopped. I suggested she might need to resume therapy since her mom had passed and I might be able to help if she would allow it. She indicated she would like me to do that.

Feeling more comfortable with her, I asked her to wait where she was so I could go to my vehicle. I was not yet sure what God was going to lead me to do but I knew I was going to assist her in some way. I found a legal pad to write my name, number and email address on to give her in case she decided she really wanted my assistance. I then moved to the back of my vehicle to select one of the four copies of Steve Arterburn's Healing Is A Choice I had purchased at the conference. I felt strongly she needed his message. While I had not yet read his book, I had met him the day before as well as heard him speak twice and knew the impact he could make if she only gave him a chance. This forlorn lady truly needed the message of hope found in his book.

I returned to the front seat of my vehicle to get my wallet out of my locked glove compartment. I rarely travel with lots of cash and was surprised to discover I still had $140 with me. A quick mental calculation told me it would likely take her two tanks of gas to get to Roanoke from where we were plus she needed money for food. I took out five $20 bills and placed them in my shirt pocket.

Before I could shut the door, I heard, "M'am," from right behind me. I turned with the book in my hand to find she had walked right up on me in spite of my request for her to remain where I had left her.

I handed her the book and said, "I think you need to read this."

She stared at it for a minute, looked up, smiled and said, "Yes, I think so, too. It looks like a good book. I'll buy a copy as soon as I get back to Roanoke."

"No," I said firmly, "I want you to take this one. I have three other copies in the car."

Crying again, she thanked me. I then gave her the paper with my personal information on it. I reiterated I believed I could help her. She said she believed it, too. I asked her to contact me as soon as she got home that night, no matter what time that was. I also told her she could email me whenever she felt up to it because I thought I could direct her to some beneficial resources.

Appearing grateful, but disappointed, I suspect she thought it would end there. I then reached into my pocket and handed her the $100. She burst into tears and asked if she could hug me. Without hesitation, I said, "Of course, you can."

"I'm a hugger," she explained.

"So am I," I replied.

She hugged me as if I were her last friend in the world. I embraced her with similar vigor. Suddenly, she yanked away from me, eyes wide open, and exclaimed, "I feel God in you."

Stunned, I whispered, "What did you just say?"

"I feel God in you. You are so at peace."

It was my turn to have eyes glistening with tears. "Thank you," I choked out.

"That's not all I see," she rushed on. "God is telling me that you are going to write a book to help women who have been sexually abused."

I leaned back against my vehicle and stared at this woman. This could be no mere chance encounter. When I could speak, I told her I had just completed a book I hoped would do just that and half the profits were dedicated to a group I volunteered with: H-E-A-R-T, Hope Exists After Rape Trauma. I went on to say it may go to the publisher in June. She shook her head in amazement and gasped, "There's no way I possibly could have known that."

"No," I allowed, "you couldn't have."

She searched me for awhile, shook her head and said, "But the book God is telling me about is a workbook which will help women who have been sexually abused. That is the book He wants you to write." I told her time would tell but felt I had just been given a directive from above.

I suggested gently it was time for us to get back on the road towards our individual destinations. She said she would be stopping at the next exit to get fuel and something to eat. She asked if I would like to join her. I told her I would love to but really needed to get home. I encouraged her to be safe, to lock her doors and to wear her seat belt. She indicated she would be sure to lock her doors as that was how she had been robbed – she had neglected to lock her doors.

I also told her to be careful who she approached as she did not know me. I said I understood she must have felt desperate as she had placed herself in a situation for something else bad to happen to her. She had certainly been through enough. She nodded in agreement, and then asked, "Would you like to know why I picked you instead of any of the others?"

"Yes, I would."

She looked me squarely in the eyes and said, "You have such a sense of peace about you."

I told her I had just experienced a very peaceful few days at the conference. I also went on to tell her I was likely more at peace in my life now than I had ever been and she would not have always been able to say that about me.

At that point, I found myself shivering – not from the cold – but from what I was coming to realize was a meeting that could have only been predestined by God. She looked at me with concern and said, "I'm sorry, you must be cold."

"No," I replied, "but I really do need to get on the road."

"About the money," she began.

"I don't want to see the money again," I insisted. "When you get on your feet again, you may meet someone down on their luck. Help them and provide them the same option. Have you ever seen the movie, *Pay It Forward*?"

"Yes, I love that movie," she exclaimed.

"I just hope you don't have to lose a child like the mother in the movie did."

"I already have," she whispered.

Thinking there was nothing I could say that would not bring up some sadness in her life, I simply said, "I'm sorry."

"It's okay," she replied. "She was only two months old."

"No matter the age, it is still a loss." I responded.

"Have you ever lost a child?" she inquired.

"My daughter was supposed to be a twin but I miscarried the twin," I said. Not knowing what else to say at this point, I said, "We really do need to get back on the road now. Call me when you get home."

"I will," she promised, "but it will be very late."

"It doesn't matter," I said, "I just would like to know you got there okay. The phone is right beside my bed and I'll be able to go right back to sleep."

"Okay," she said. We hugged again before she walked to her car. I watched her get into her car before I got into my Escape. I allowed her to pull out ahead of me. She exited the ramp much like Dr. Brown's Delorean in *Back to the Future,* almost leaving me to wonder if the encounter was real.

I would love to tell you she called me to tell me she arrived home safely. It has been more than two years and I have heard nothing. I can only pray she is okay and receiving the assistance she needs.

Several times while we were talking that night, she told me I had changed her life forever. As I have reflected on our interlude on I-95, I realize it was she who changed mine.

For two years, I have struggled with the book she said God wanted me to write. Just recently, I began writing it. It is entitled Cries in the Dark and will be the next book I publish, God willing.

jbh

REAL TESTIMONIES

As I was preparing the testimony
I'm scheduled to deliver in a few weeks
I was suddenly struck by a different perspective
About testimonies, in general,
And what lasting impact, if any, they might have
On people who either hear or read them:
When I consider my own story
I realize some may be shocked,
Others momentarily moved to tears,
Some impacted for the short-term
While others may decide to champion
The organization for which I volunteer
Because they now place a familiar face
With the needs of others with similar stories

Still, real testimonies are not made of mere words
But by our every day actions
Whether or not others are watching
As that is how each of us should really be measured:
Did we take the time to help someone today ~
Someone who did not know us
Who could not possibly further our careers
Or repay us in any way?

Did we return the extra change given us
By the cashier who may just lose his job
When the drawer comes up short at day's end
Or did we pocket the difference
Then brag about it to our family and friends?
Did we sleep in instead of going to church
Because we were too tired or the weather was bad
Yet sent our children to school in similar
        circumstances

Since education is important to their future?
Yes, the real testimonies in our lives
Are not the messages we give from pulpits in
        churches
Or from lecterns in auditoriums or lecture halls
Nor are they those we write for magazines and books.

Real testimonies are found in all the ways
We strive to be more like Christ
In our thoughts and our deeds,
In our willingness to stand up for what is right
And not roll over for what we know to be wrong.

So, while the words of my testimony
May touch the lives of a few for a while
It is my fervent prayer the way I live my life
Is the real testimony that will touch others
So they, too, will want to know more
About this Savior named Jesus, the Christ.

        jbh
      1-17-06

Precious Child

Precious child, eyes aglow
Innocently reaching for one
Whose hand's always there
No matter the urgency of her need.

She emanates the security
Of one who's loved,
Needs and wants met,
Happy in her environment.

How is it this child already
Demonstrates the total trust
Each Christian should display
When anchored in a relationship with God?

Is she too young to be distracted
By the realities of the world
Thereby focusing on the one
Who provides her every need?

No wonder our Savior said,
"Permit the children to come to me…
The kingdom of God
Belongs to such as these."[1]

Precious children reach out to Him
Trusting He will meet their needs ~
To live abundantly like them
We must simply follow their lead.

> jbh
> 8-12-07

---

[1]   Mark 10:14

Be Mindful of Demons

Be mindful of those demons
Advice which you must heed
To avoid mindlessly slipping into
Some misbegotten deed
So foreign from your nature
Most people will exclaim
Whatever possessed her
To chance ruining her good name?

The way a man is thinking
Describes who he is, I'm told,
It's really those things, on which he dwells,
That shed light on his soul;
For from all hearts come evil thoughts
It says so in the Word
Quoted straight from Lord Jesus
The greatest teacher ever heard.

The enemy is not happy
When for God we work
He will take most anything
To make us sin, then smirk
When we begin to doubt our worth
Even wonder if we're sane
Begin to erode our confidence
Cause us undue pain;

Satan knows our every weakness,
Comes for us when we're so tired,
Turn away from his temptations
For Christ, you must be wired,
Ask Him to fight your demons,
Tell Him about your sin,
Pray for His forgiveness
With Him, you'll always win.

jbh
6-26-07

Revival, 2007

Precious Lord, we gather this evening
As a church searching for purpose;
One splintered by past hurts –
Some with boils that will not heal
While others have forgiven and moved on –
All in need of a mighty revival
To cleanse minds, hearts and spirits,
Uniting us in one purpose,
Saving souls for Christ.

How perfectly timed, this revival, Father,
Two weeks after the celebration of
The resurrection of Your only begotten Son,
Our risen Savior, the only hope for the future;
A time for renewing commitments,
For sharing His unconditional love
With lost and lonely souls
Found within and without church walls.

Prepare us for revival, Lord,
By cleansing hearts and minds
As we gather in Your name;
Teach us this week
To respond more like Your Son –
Reaching and teaching all who need Him,
Modeling His love in all we say and do
No matter the circumstances.

Revive us, Holy Father,
Renew us, we beseech Thee,
Open our ears to Your word,
Our hearts to Your direction,
Our hands and feet to Your will;

Lift our voices to sing Your praises,
Bend our knees to pray for change
That will energize our members
To become Your ambassadors, Lord.
Oh, bless this revival, we pray!

jbh
4-19-07

WHERE WILL YOUR BEACON LEAD?

I'm never quite sure
Where Your beacon will lead
But I've learned every time
I step outside its warm glow
I become disoriented
Finding myself listening to voices
Not guided by similar values
Wanting nothing better
Than to persuade me
You removed Your light
While things were going well
Leaving me to scramble desperately
Whenever life soured.

This truth remains constant:
I am the one who strays
Once the storm clouds pass
Making Your beacon seem
Less radiant in contrast
To the sun shining brilliantly.
My God, do I simply forget
You provide the beacons of night
And the sun of day
In addition to all our needs?

So as I look toward Your beacon
To chart the direction of my newest journey
I remind myself of the importance
Of remaining clearly focused
On the tasks You set before me
Being careful not to imagine
 I can be successful
Through any of my actions
But only those You choose for me.

        jbh
    12-16-05

Prayer Questions

Arms raised to heaven
  in praise of God;
    to receive the Savior's embrace;
      to go hand-in-hand with a loved one
        waiting to escort you to heaven?

Compelled to pray
words escape me
as your countenance transitions
  from excruciating pain
    to a modicum of relief
      then a sense of peace.

Only one unselfish supplication exists:
  Father, God, bestow your mercy,
    grace and love upon her;
      Heal her as only You can,
        Lord, I beseech you ...

"Janice!"
"Janice, I need you!"
Revelry broken, I go to her
  attending to her needs;
    wanting to understand her desires;
      loving her more than ever.

Needs met, she dozes again
leaving me to reflect anew
on purposeful prayer
knowing the inevitable is near.

Lord, you know my heart,
my selfish desires
meet my needs,
not hers;

Father, I beseech you:
bestow your compassion and mercy
as she completes this final journey;
provide me the grace and courage
to let her go in peace.
Your word, Lord, promises
comfort for the broken-hearted,
strength for the weak,
grace beyond all understanding,
reunion for those who
confess their sins,
believe in Christ, Jesus,
affirm Him as Lord and Savior.

She's in Your hands, God,
as she's always been,
as your plan unfolds
teach me
your timing,
your ways,
your will.
Thank you, Father, for
years shared,
lessons taught,
unconditional love,
irrevocable memories,
faithful assurances,
eternal connections
Amen

jbh
12-30-06

<u>Only On Our Knees</u>

Only on our knees
Do we find you, Lord,
For it is there that
       eyes open
           hearts break
               wills yield
                    fears pour forth
               weaknesses show
           ears hear
       truths become known
Although often neglected because
Minds are swayed
By earthly pleasures
Instead of eternal goals.

On my knees, Father,
I am closer to You
Than any other time
For it is then
       I block out the world
           open my soul
               solely Yours
                    surrounded by Your love
               talking with my Savior
           filled with Your spirit
       awaiting Your word
To lead me on the path You've chosen
As You teach discernment and discipleship.

On our knees, Lord,
Too often one-sided dialogues
Instead of conversations as we share
  our struggles
    wants and needs
      fears and dreams
        even confessions
  rarely giving thanks
    much less praise
  for mercy and grace

Oh, loving Father, give us discernment to know
How to communicate with You when we are
On our knees.

   jbh
   7-22-07

Going to Zarephath

You want me to do what?
God, please!
Walk away from my life's work
To pursue a future known only to You?

Trust you?
Of course, but ...
Do it.
Not now, Lord –
It's all I know,
      What I do,
            Who I am.

What?
The mirror?
Why, God?
Can't you see it?
Of course, but you know why, Lord:
      Illness,
            Loss,
                  Fatigue,
                        Deadlines ...
What do you expect?

Obey me!
But, Lord, I ...
Have faith?
Of course I do.
Show me!

I try, Father, by
>Praying,
>>Worshipping,
>>>Doing good works;

I believe You are
>Creator of heaven and earth;
In Jesus as our Lord and Savior
>And in the Holy Spirit.

Trust me!
But I do, God, I do.
Do as I have commanded.
Retire?
Absolutely.
Now?
Yes, I have plans for you.
What plans, Lord?
In my time, my child.
Great.
It will be, I promise.
Four more years, God, please.
I've already waited three.
Do what I say,
Great will be your reward.

Like Elijah, God sent me to Zarephath,
Introduced me to the widow
Who put faith into action
Forever changing her life
To give me the same challenge.

I saw,

    Heard,

        Believed,

            Retired –

                Health Improved,

            Had time for others

Walked with God

Jesus in me

    Freedom

        Serenity

            Peace

                Found in Zarephath.

       jbh: 11-19-06

Resurrection, Sunday Morn

Air crisp and cool as I arrive
At church this glorious Easter
Sun rising in the east
Moon full in the west
Barely lighting the lone cross
Draped with the white shroud
Representing our resurrected Lord
Who left that tomb empty for
Mary and Martha to discover on
That third day after His death—
His crucifixion on Calvary's Hill.

Tears fill my eyes, spilling over
As I listen to age-old scripture
Which foretold what Christ would suffer
Even before King David was born
Then stand in awe at how we,
Twenty centuries later, are as thrilled
As Mary, Martha and the disciples to hear
"He is risen! He is risen! He is risen!"
The words that electrify the hearts of all believers.

Jesus' life would mean nothing today
If you and I could visit His grave
For that would make Him just another man,
A good man, even a perfect man,
But not the One we call Savior.
Without that empty tomb, we are
Condemned to eternal damnation
Instead, we're saved by His Resurrection.
Praise God for His amazing grace and outrageous
Love!

jbh
3-23-08

I'm Free

Words spoken
Shackles broken
I'm free
Finally free.

My story
God's glory
I'm free
Finally free.

You defamed me
God reclaimed me
I'm free
Finally free.

As lies unfolded
God remolded
I'm free
Finally free.

You'd waiver
Not my Savior
I'm free
Finally free.

What you tore
Jesus bore
I'm free
Finally free.

Sound the alarms
I'm in God's arms
I'm free
Finally free.

No more doubting
Simply shouting
I'm free
Finally free.

Satan, go away
This is God's day
I'm free
Finally free.

No more feeling?
Come for healing
Be free
Finally free.

Let your story
Become God's glory
Be free
Finally free.

Ceremonies
Testimonies
Be free
Finally free.

jbh
2-15-06

<u>Could It Be?</u>

Awesome plan
Gone askew
Could it be
Wasn't meant for you?

Trying to sleep
Quarter past two
Could it be
God's talking to you?

Early morning
Rushing to school
Morning prayer
Wasn't cool!

Time for lunch
Time for play
Time for work
But not to pray.

Someone's shooting
Someone's dead
Suppose it'd been
You instead?

His glorious plan
Meant for you
Freely given
Wouldn't come true -

Didn't accept
His precious gift
Detours with Satan
Set you adrift.

Daily talks with God
Have made me see
Eternity's available
For one such as me

Reach for Him
It's not too late
Could it be
It'll change your fate?

jbh
8-2-07

Could It Be evolved one night when I was having difficulty sleeping. I sat up in bed, surrounded by my two Scotties, Gwen and Mac, and began making notes on how to divide this book into sections. I knew I wanted to include a variety of reflections on each sub-topic and decided to list those. Meanwhile, my pups decided to go back to sleep. As I wrote, the line "could it be" kept dancing in my head. Knowing I would not be able to sleep until the line was dealt with, I completed the first task, placed my pen on a blank sheet of paper and waited for God's guidance.

One could substitute any situation that would cause someone to have a premature death—premature in this case meaning dying prior to accepting Jesus Christ as one's Lord and Savior. If you have not yet done that, I pray you will do it now. It is a four-part process that will forever change your life:

1. Admit you are a sinner.
2. Ask for forgiveness.
3. Believe Jesus Christ died on the Cross for your sins, rose from the grave, and ascended into heaven.
4. Through prayer, receive Jesus Christ as your Lord and Savior thereby giving Him control of your life through the Holy Spirit.

If you don't know what to pray, you may want to use this prayer:

Dear Lord Jesus:

I know I am a sinner and am in need of your forgiveness. I believe You died for my sins, rose from the grave, and ascended into Heaven. I want to give up my sins. I invite You to come into my heart and take control of my life. I give You my trust and want to follow You as Lord and Savior.

In Your Most Holy Name,
Amen

Family

"No matter what you've done for yourself or for humanity, if you can't look back on having given love and attention to your own family, what have you really accomplished?" – Lee Iacocca

<u>Mom</u>

If I could give you just one thing
Which would show what you mean to me
I'd share what I find each time I enter your door:
        a sense of welcome
        a feeling of security
        a state of well-being

I know no matter what I do
I can always enter that door
        unannounced
        unafraid
Knowing whatever trouble I have
You shall share it willingly
And whatever good news I have
You will rejoice and smile with me

No matter where I go or what I do
I will never be able to repay you
Nor will I ever forget you
Thank you, Mom, for also being my friend

      jbh

I Love You

I love you—
How simple those three words often seem
Yet, when spoken from the heart
Become the reason for living,
For continuing when life gets tough,
For waking in the morning
And turning in at night
For doing, with feeling,
All those things which have become trivial

I love you—
Words that give strength,
Renew faith in ourselves,
And make living much more
Than the metamorphosis from birth to death,
Keeping us from merely existing

I love you—
Don't really understand why
But the reasons
Aren't nearly as important as the fact;
Just know I do;
Regard it as the one thing in life
Of which you can be certain

For to stop
Would turn my life
Into mere existence,
Without purpose,
Not worth living—
I love life,
I love you!

jab
1-26-72

When Duty Calls

Sometimes I think I've lost you
Then I realize it's only my mind playing tricks
For you're gone out of duty
Not lost hopes or dreams
We'll be together again
When our nation calls less urgently
Knowing that, I spend time working
To see good in what's happening
Most often finding only the despair we both feel
Neither able to accept or change what must be
Yet, we should and possibly could
If fear didn't lurk in the back of our minds
Ever present, although futile
We'll each change while you're gone
Of that we can be sure
We must pray our years of knowing and loving
Will make change work for, not against, us–
It is with this I leave you
A pledge of love which time may alter
But never destroy.

                    jbh
                    12-2-74

Cindy

For thirty years I lived without you
        five of them believing you were beyond my grasp
Then, wondrously, when I least suspected it,
        she discovered you within me
        making me complete even before I knew I wasn't

In the midst of pain I found a joy
        that even now I can barely express
        who would have guessed you were there
        in the midst of my turmoil
        turning my despair into jubilation

Then came that shaky period when
        I was required to make a decision—
        the terrifying decision—
        to keep you full-term or let you go

Yet, from the start, I knew I had to chance it
        had to trust there was a reason
        for your being within me
        defying all odds
        and God, in His infinite wisdom,
        was testing if I truly desired you

The choice was simple
        I would have you
        no matter the cost
And when I heard your first heartbeat
        all my fears were dispelled
        I knew I'd made the only choice
        with which I could live

Suddenly, it was September 5, 1981,
    I saw you for the first time
    vigorously sucking your thumb,
    the most beautiful baby girl I'd ever seen

Instantly, I realized the true essence of love—
    Cindy, my beautiful little girl,
    I know whatever may occur
    in my remaining years
No experience will ever match the day
    you came into my life

        Forever unconditional love,
        Mom

    jbh
    5-18-82

Arlene Ruth Brown

It all began
One sunny day
When they brought to you
A Wanda Kay;
She was the start
Of the many joys
Of all the little
Girls and boys.

But, ah, if memory
Serves me well
They all weren't little
I'm here to tell;
In fact, some Johns,
And a Melvin, too,
Were some of those
They brought to you.

A Butch, a Kathy,
A Richard, who
Is glad to say
Is still with you;
And some so special
In the group
They've come back home
To eat your soup.

Do you remember
That last wee girl
Who set our hearts
In such a whirl?

And, even though
There's only two
Who can truly say
They came from you
There's twenty-three
Who're glad to say
You were their mom
For many a day.

And, so, to you
We give a toast
'Cause you're a mom
Who's simply the most!

jbh
5-22-84

Interview With Grandma

Born in the land of Lincoln
Was a little girl named Arlene
Because she was cripple
There were many things she hadn't seen.
Do onto others the way you want to be treated
Is what her mother always said;
Roosevelt made a plan
To pay for medication for the sick ones in bed.
To school she would wear a dress
That came below the knee
Boys would wear suits
How cute that would be.
Her favorite foods both now and then
Include shrimp and spaghetti
So stay in school and study hard
So you can get a job and be ready.

Cindy Holland
1995

While interviewing my grandma, she became very emotional while
talking about her mother. On other questions, she answered with
a laugh or put much emphasis on an answer. She was happy to do
the interview for me.

You

I look at you
and all I see
is an empty shell
of what used to be

I speak to you
but you can't hear
the anguish and pain
that's always there

I reach for you
but you don't feel
how long it's been
since it's been real

It's so sad
you can't see
your loss of self
is killing me

Yet, I'll move on
because I must
and find some help
from those I trust

But this I pledge
with you I'll stay
and on my knees
each day I'll pray

One day soon
you'll once more be
the kind of man
who married me.

jbh
9-13-00

Gwen & Mac

Scampering over the
Carpet
Onto the
Tables
Turning flips
Impish
Silly pups
Hotfooting about the house

Terrors
Erupting
Round the
Rose bushes outside
Inside
Everything is
Run over by them

Twin
Wreckers
In
No
Skid paws

> jbh
> 12-14-07

Pets are very important members of our families!

When Dad Left

Almost six months ago today
You left for a better place
While the tears often freely flow
I don't wear them in disgrace

I never really thought
I'd have to face the day
I would no longer have you
To help me find my way

We promised you those last few days
We would each be all right
But none of us have found a way
To always maintain the fight

Before you left you looked at me
And said you loved me so
I knew right then I'd have to find
A way to let you go

So through the night I held your hand
With my other on your heart
So I knew the very moment
From this earth you did depart

There'll never be another one
Who'll know me quite as well
And there are still so many things
I wish for you to tell

So, as I sit here and reflect
Somberly beside your grave
I find I'm ever so grateful
For all the things you gave

And while today has found me
Just a wee bit more than sad
I'll be forever grateful
God picked you as my dad

jbh
11-21-02

Marriage Trials

I say neither wants to be the first to say good-bye
You say neither has the nerve to say hello –
My heart jumps at the possibilities to which
That simple assessment could lead

Praying for a troubled marriage
You implore God to place us on a path
Of improved communications, reconnections,
Or some form of comfortable companionship

Seriously doubting my ability to heal past wounds,
To learn to trust, share, love, or care enough
To make this marriage work,
I know vows repeated long ago require the effort

A knock on the door while in conference
       "You have a call…"
       "They said it's important!"
       "Yes?"
"Broken nose? Meet him where?
         E.R.?
       "It's pretty bad."
       "How bad can a broken nose be?"
       "Is she coming?"
       "I'm on my way!"

Hurts, disappointments, miscommunications disappear
Meaningless when the person one loves
Is brought in on a gurney with
Fourteen life-threatening facial fractures

Amazing how God uses tragedies to awaken us
Making us realize what's important
While there's still time to make things work
Without having a lifetime of regrets

jbh: 3-31-03

As You Lay Dying

I sit and watch
As you struggle to breathe
Mouth wide open
Eyes fixed on something or someone
Seen only by you
It is obvious pain persists
In cramping legs which
No longer offer you support
Making you totally dependent
On someone else for your needs
Your bones crack loudly as we move you
Causing you to cry in pain ~
We apologize for hurting you
But you say you're sorry
For putting us through this
You've stopped eating now
Drinking only ice water
To take medications that
Seem to stem the onslaught
Of those torturous cramps
You stated yesterday
You're ready to go home ~
When asked where that was
You made it crystal clear
It's the heavenly one you desire
You rarely talk any more
About things in the present
Rather, you constantly ask if
Daddy is okay and we answer that
He's resting peacefully now
I don't know how much longer
You'll continue suffering
In this halfway house
Somehow stuck in neutral
Between this world and the next

I can only pray
God will soon bestow
His utmost mercy and grace by
Releasing you from your earthly pain
Allowing you to enter those Pearly Gates

                    jbh
          9-19-03

A Promise Is A Promise

It was the spring of my Junior year of college when my world felt as if it were falling apart. I lost my grandfather that March. We had always shared a special bond. You see, I grew up next door to my grandparents. I guess you could say they spoiled me. I was the youngest and the only granddaughter of their three grandchildren. I spent a lot of time with my grandparents while growing up. Losing my grandfather was like losing a part of myself. It didn't help that I was five hours away at the time.

Not long after my grandfather's death, my grandmother's health started to decline. The two had always been close and they sort of supported each other, so we knew when one died, the other might follow soon after. Grandma began falling a lot at home. She already had problems with her heart and we feared her falls were a sign the problem was worsening.

Throughout my senior year of college, grandma had her ups and downs. Each time I was able to go home, I spent time with her. We would talk about sports and school and she would update me on the town news. I enjoyed every minute I spent with her.

In the spring of my senior year, my boyfriend picked me up from class and told me we had to go right home. I knew something was wrong, and my instincts told me it was bad. He said my grandma was in the hospital and it was not looking good. He had already packed my bag so we left straight from the parking lot—yet another horrible five hour trip! I wanted to get there so badly. I talked to each of my family members by phone on the way home. It was so hard not being there. I was afraid I would not get to say goodbye.

When we got to the hospital, mom prepared me for the worst. She said the doctors told her only 20% of grandma's heart was working. They were discussing surgery but there was a chance she would not survive. This was devastating news as within a year I had just lost one of my favorite people and it appeared I was about to lose another. Additionally, it was Easter weekend and grandma's birthday was in three days. It did not look like there was going to be much celebrating this year. After what seemed like an eternity of waiting, the doctors decided to proceed with the surgery. I was scared to death, fearing I was about to lose my grandma any minute. My family and I prayed for the best with our preacher. I was allowed to visit with her briefly before they took her to the operating room. She smiled when she saw me and indicated things were not looking too good. I told her she was being silly and everything would work out fine. She grabbed my hand as I gave her a kiss and let her know that I loved her. I was so terrified this would be the last exchange between the "girls".

Mom talked to me a lot during the wait. I asked why they decided on the surgery. She said grandma told the doctors I would be graduating from college in May and she had promised she would be there. She insisted the doctor make it so she could keep her promise and if the surgery was the only way she could do that, she would have it. I could not believe she had done this. It is one of the most special things anyone had ever done for me. I just hugged my mom and we both cried.

Grandma survived the surgery. She let the doctor know he now had to get her ready for her trip. He could not believe she was serious. Graduation was in two weeks. There was no way she would be ready to make a five hour trip that soon. She reminded him it was the agreement they had made before she signed for her operation. She set her jaw firmly and reminded him she had a promise to keep and she intended to keep it.

On graduation day, I was the happiest girl there. I had all of my favorite people around to watch me graduate—my parents, uncle, boyfriend, best friend, and best of all, my grandma. To me, she looked better than I had ever seen her. I ran over to give her a big hug before the ceremony began. She gave me a kiss and told me I better know how much she loved me. I told her I sure did and gave her another hug.

Grandma kept her promise. She saw me graduate. Two weeks later, she had to enter hospice care. It happened to be my first day back home when the final paperwork had to be completed. It was then the impact of what she had done for me really sunk in. It was very hard accepting how much pain she was in. I felt if she had not come to see me graduate things would have been better for her. This was one of the hardest things I'd ever had to overcome and I'm still working on it.

Throughout the summer I watched grandma slowly deteriorate. When August approached, I did not want to return to school. Grandma was getting worse and I could not bear the thought of another long trip. I would be entering a new school that was two hours farther away than my undergraduate school. I could not even stand to think what an emergency seven hour trip home would be like.

I left for school while making my mom promise to keep me updated, good or bad. I did not want to be left in the clouds during any of this. She said she would keep me posted. I went back into the house to give my grandma one final kiss before leaving. Yet again, I left wondering if this would be the last exchange we would have.

I would call to check up on grandma from school. Sometimes it was hard talking to her because she was losing her memory. She would think she was talking to my mom and in the middle of the conversation she would realize she was talking to me again. It was so hard seeing her go like this. I did not want to think about my grandma like that; she was the best; and I just could not bear it.

In October, that dreaded phone call came. Mom told me they did not expect grandma to live through the next day. The seven hour trip seemed longer than ever and I hated every minute of it. I hated myself for going away to school and leaving her.

When I arrived home, I was not prepared for how bad my grandma had gotten. Tears filled my eyes when I saw her. She was unable to speak due to a stroke she suffered on Monday of that week. I leaned over to tell her how much I loved her and that I was there. It was so hard not hearing her say it back. It was the first time in my life that had ever happened.

I sat with her as much as I could until her final minutes. I did not want to let her go. Although she had not responded to anyone in several days, a single tear slid down her face when I kissed her goodnight and told her I loved her one last time. It was her way of letting me know she had heard me.

That was last semester. I still have yet to fully overcome my grief of either grandparent. It was a very difficult year and a half for my family and me. We learned how close our family is and what it really means to be a family. I learned the biggest lesson of all. *A promise is a promise* and I will fight till death to keep it.

Cindy Holland
2004

Sometimes I

Sometimes the best parts of my day
       are the few minutes I get alone with you
       those times we share with no one
Sometimes I tell you serious things
       you just watch me with eyes wide open
Sometimes I tell you silly stuff
       so you laugh at your giggling mom
Sometimes I watch as you sleep
       and wish you'd always be that peaceful
Sometimes I teach you crazy things
       for you to share with dad
       then he believes we've both lost it
       but loves us both the same
Sometimes I just watch you play
       and relax for, in many instances,
       the first time during the day
Sometimes I watch you stare at things
       and wonder what is it you see
       what is really spinning through
       that little head of yours
Always when I watch you
       I wonder about your future
       and make a silent vow
       to always be here for you
No matter what happens in our lives
       I will continue to enjoy watching you
       and will always love you unconditionally

      jbh
      5-18-82

Bless This House

I sit in this huge, empty house built by my father
So my mother's parents could move from California
Over forty-two years ago

A labor of love for his wife who moved south
Where she knew no one other than him
At the end of World War II

Living in centuries' old farm houses most of their
      marriage
My parents moved into this house
Upon the death of my grandmother

Grandma's last ride from here was by Rescue Squad
Which took her to the hospital where she died
A few hours later

My mom's last ride from here was in a hearse
Which took her to the funeral home
In preparation for our final good-byes

I was with each of them as they left this room
Where I now sit trying to make sense of it all
Deciding what my next steps should be

As a child, I walked over from the farm next door
      with my mom
As she dreamed out loud what it would be like
To have her parents living next door

My parents were about to move in with Grandma
As she became more and more feeble
Bur she was unable to wait for them

Maybe that made it easier for mom and dad

To make changes for this to become their home
Than it will be for my husband and me

Two generations of my family have lived here
But neither lived with the generation before
As I have over the last few years

How do I separate the caretaker role from the
      homemaker one
To become the third generation to enhance my
      father's handiwork
And make it a home instead of a shrine

How do I walk through this room and not see the bed
Where mom laid for months in her own private hell
And not continue to feel the pain of her loss

What do I do with the Christmas tree which stood
      fully decorated
In this room from December 2002 to provide earthly
      light
For mom's passage into eternal light in October 2003

What do I do with the emptiness which pervades
      every phase of my life
Even as I attempt not to withdraw into myself or
Fall into habits I know are self-destructive

I know it is too soon to have answers—
I need to be patient as I try to sort all this
With the assistance of those who know me best

Just as all this transpired in God's time and way
I must continue to listen for His voice in all I do
Remembering He is omnipotent and all-loving

This house may become my home and the home
Of my child, her children, and her grandchildren
If I can make the proper decisions

If the next generation of my family is able to make
        this house a home
Worthy of passing on to future generations
What a tribute that would be to my father

jbh
11-17-03

Daddy's Little Girl

Why am I always pushed away,
     like some chore to be saved for another day?
We used to be so close
     yet now I feel like you're setting me loose.
You were always there for me,
lending a helping hand and showing me how to be
Now we argue and fight
     And I know this can't be right
I don't understand just what I did
     But you have to understand
          I'm not a kid
     I'm older now, but I want you to know
     I still need you with me
To love and to grow
I guess what I'm trying to ask is
     Whatever happened to Daddy's Little Girl?

     Cindy Holland
     1985

Ride Like The Wind

"Mommy, can we go to the farm for my birthday so I can ride Granddaddy's new horse?" six-year-old Arlene asked her mom.

"It depends on how the weather is, Honey," her mom replied. "You know we still get snow around here in April sometimes. Besides, it's not even Thanksgiving yet. Why are you asking about that now?"

"Because Granddad said it would take a few months before he would have Comanche tame enough for me to ride. Even if we go there during Christmas break, I won't be able to ride him. That's why I want to go back for my birthday. Please, Mommy, please..."

"We'll see, Sweetheart. Now get ready for bed."

"Ok, Mommy. Is Daddy going to be home from work before I go to bed?"

"No, Arlene. You know he can't leave the bowling alley until all the leagues are done for the night. You ask me that every time it's time for bed. Why do you think the answer is going to change?" her mom asked.

Arlene pouted. "I just wish he could tuck me into bed once in a while."

"Well, if your dad didn't have this job, there'd be no money to drive to Granddaddy's farm in Wisconsin any time. Then you'd never even get to *see* his new horse much less ride it. Jobs are hard to come by these days, little girl. You need to learn to be thankful."

"Yes, ma'am. I'm sorry, Mommy. Give Daddy a kiss for me when he gets home, ok?"

"Yes, dear." She tucked Arlene into bed. "You sleep tight now."

It was November, 1933. Arlene's father worked in a bowling alley, setting up pins after each bowler rolled a ball. Her mom was a bookkeeper for a financial agency. Although they were not destitute, there was not a lot of money for extras. The family would likely have to forego the Christmas trip to Wisconsin if Arlene wanted to go in April for her birthday. Dorothy and Raymond, Arlene's parents, would have to discuss that while Arlene was at school so she would not be able to cut in on their conversation.

Raymond arrived home around midnight. "How are my two favorite girls?" he asked Dorothy as he kissed her lightly on the cheek.

"Fine," Dorothy responded. "Arlene's making a fuss again about your not being home to tuck her in at night."

"That little scamp. I guess I'll just have to go in and give her a kiss good night now."

Dorothy laughed. "That's fine, but don't you dare wake up that child. You know we have a devil of a time getting her back to sleep if she is awakened during the night."

Raymond tiptoed into Arlene's room to give her a kiss on her forehead. He noticed she was moaning in her sleep and appeared to be restless. When he leaned down to kiss her, he realized she was very warm. Alarmed, he called Dorothy into the room.

"Ray, what's wrong with you? I thought I asked you not to wake Arlene."

By the time Dorothy got to the room, Raymond had turned the light on to get a better look at his daughter. She was extremely flushed and fidgety. He laid his hand against her cheek. "Dorothy, she's very warm. You come feel her."

Dorothy moved over to the bed and felt Arlene's neck. Sure enough, Arlene was feverish. Dorothy motioned for Raymond to get the thermometer so they could take her temperature. When Dorothy placed her cool hand on her daughter's forehead, Arlene struggled to open her eyes.

"Mommy, I don't feel so good."

"What's wrong, Honey?"

"I'm burning up, my head hurts, my whole body hurts. Mooommmmy, what's wrong with me?"

"I don't know, Sweetheart. Let me take your temperature, and then we'll call the doctor, okay?"

"Do you have to call the doctor?"

"Let's see what your temperature is first, and then we'll decide."

Raymond came rushing in with the thermometer, shaking it down so it would register properly. He placed it under Arlene's tongue and helped her keep it in place for several minutes until he was sure it had registered.

"Dorothy, this child's temperature is 103.5°! We've got to call for help right away."

Dorothy called their pediatrician and explained the sudden onslaught of symptoms. He suggested it would be wise to take Arlene straight to the hospital as he had been seeing quite a few cases of Scarlet Fever recently and did not want to take any chances. He encouraged her to bundle Arlene up as tightly as possible so she would not get pneumonia on top of whatever ailment she might already have.

* *

"Doctor, it's been more than twenty-four hours. Can't you tell us anything?" Arlene's parents were frantic with worry.

"As I suspected when we talked on the phone, Arlene has a severe case of Scarlet Fever. The next forty-eight hours are going to be very crucial. You need to try to get some rest," the doctor said as gently as he could.

Raymond yelled at the doctor: "How the hell am I supposed to rest when out of the blue my only child is critically ill? She was fine when I left for work yesterday. I come home and she has some strange fever. Could you rest if she was your child?"

"Calm down, Mr. Edwards. We're doing all we can for her. The best thing we can do now is wait and pray."

* *

On the second night, the Intensive Care Unit nurse came out to get Arlene's parents. "The doctors need to see both of you right away."

"Nooooooooo," Dorothy cried. "Arlene can't be dead!"

"Oh, no," reassured the nurse. "The doctors just want to talk to both of you."

They entered the unit where Arlene lay very pale and still. The doctors walked away from her so she wouldn't overhear their conversation with her parents. "Mr. and Mrs. Edwards, we think it's time you contact your parents and anyone else you might like to have here should your daughter not make it through the night. She's no longer responding to the medicines. We've done all we can for her."

"I refuse to accept that," Dorothy stated. "Arlene is going to ride her grandfather's horse, Comanche, in April, as part of her birthday present. She is going to live! I'm sure she's dreaming about that day right now."

"That's a nice thought, Mrs. Edwards, but we just don't see that happening. You need to prepare yourself for the worst. I'm very sorry."

Dorothy collapsed into Raymond's arms, sobbing uncontrollably. "God's not going to take my little girl away. I know He's not!"

"Yes, dear," was all Raymond could utter. The only solace he could provide his wife through the night was to hold her gently while they anxiously waited for better news.

About 3:30 a.m., Dorothy and Raymond were awakened by the sound of something clanging on the floor. Startled, they jumped off the cots the hospital had provided and hurried over to Arlene's side. They were amazed to find her sitting upright for the first time since she had been admitted to the hospital. A small tray that had been left on her bed had been knocked to the floor by her sudden movement.

"Mommy, I'm hungry," Arlene cried weakly.

About that time, a nurse came running into the room. "Oh, my gosh, it's a miracle! I've got to go call the doctor immediately."

"Mommy, I'm tired. I've got to lie back down now."

"It's ok, Arlene. We love you."

"I love you, too. Daddy, you got off work to tuck me in!"

"Yes, Darling, I'm here to tuck you in. Now get some rest. I'll still be here when you wake up."

* *

Arlene's nurse was right. Arlene was a miracle. When she sat up, for reasons unknown, the Scarlet Fever "seed" bypassed her heart and settled in her hip, causing her to be crippled for the remainder of her life. She was never able to ride her granddaddy's horse, Comanche; however, she was able to visit him whenever her parents could afford the trip to Wisconsin.

Arlene spent eighteen months in a body-cast in a Shriner's Hospital as a result of her Scarlet Fever ordeal. Her parents never treated her as if she was handicapped. They made her as normal a child as possible. She played high school basketball and played the bass violin in her school band. The illness took away many of her physical abilities, but it never dampened her spirit.

* *

Arlene was married for almost 58 years; raised two children of her own and twenty-one foster children. When she died on October 25, 2003, I feel certain her grandfather had ole Comanche saddled up for her so she could finally "Ride Like the Wind." When I saw a picture of a child dreaming of her horses running in the wind, I knew I had to write her story.

* *

Arlene Ruth Edwards Brown was one of the most wonderful characters I have ever known. She was my mother.

jbh
10-2008

* *

This story won First Place in Fanstory.com's Strong Character's contest in October, 2008.

For My Parents

I am inexplicably drawn to this spot
Where your earthly remains
Lie side by side —
Lives forever bound by sixty year old vows

I talk to you
To once again feel your presence
As if unaware
You have never truly been here

For reasons I can't fathom
I can't seem to release you
Even though I wouldn't have desired
Another moment of pain for either of you

I remain transfixed as if you could
Wipe my tears
Soothe my heart
Share those wonderful smiles uniquely yours

Today I am overwhelmed with grief
For no apparent reason –
It's not an anniversary of anything
Simply another day without you

Another day when I yearn to chat
Share my victories
Discuss my defeats
Knowing each is important to you

My heart aches for you
In spite of my belief
In a hereafter
Where we will be forever rejoined

My mind rails against the knowledge
I'll not see or hear you
Until Gabrielle once again
Blows his triumphant horn

I force myself to leave this spot
To return to a world
Which seems so vacant
Without your physical presence

Maybe the pain of your loss
Will never subside
The wound
May never heal

Yet, to not have known and loved you
Would have been a far greater loss:
Somehow I know
That is the reality of this day

jbh
9-29-04

<u>So Many Questions</u>

How did we come to this juncture in life?
How long has it been since I could see
      the man I married many years ago?
When did I stop believing in our love –
      not only for you as my husband
      but also for whom I believed I was as your wife?
When did I stop respecting you both as a person
      and as the man I swore to honor
      for better or worse until death do us part?
Why am I both angered and saddened
      when I realize I now need to take care of you?
What can our daughter's view of marriage be
      after the example we've set all these years?
Is she mature enough to understand how it feels
      to watch someone you've loved your entire life
      self-destruct because he failed to continue growing
      personally and professionally leaving him unable
      to deal effectively in a world he no longer
      understands?
It must pain her deeply to watch her beloved father
      withdrawing from the harsh realities of life
      believing he has sacrificed the past thirty-one years
      so I could climb the administrative ladder.
Would it be a violation of his trust and faith to
      consider walking away when he needs me most?
How do I help him find his way to a peace of mind
      he's likely never had?
What will it take for him to hit rock bottom,
      forcing him to begin the long, arduous search
      for the healing balm which is so freely provided
      by Jehovah Rapha?

Can I be his life preserver until he can learn to swim
        on his own without the risk of both of us drowning
        in the quagmire of his depression?
What if I've spent too much time blaming him for
        what he isn't instead of honoring him for who he is
        thereby destroying the foundation of all he could
        have been, would have been,
        if only I had known?
If only I had known what?
So many questions
Too few answers
What if......?

                    jbh
                    11-2-04

<u>You, My Child, Upon Your Graduation</u>

You, my miracle child,
Nearly aborted because some said, "Not possible!"
Protected by God's own hand that led the doctor
To change the order of surgery
Allowing the discovery of your ten week old fetus
Resting snugly in my womb

You, my only child,
Born healthy in spite of odds
So strongly stacked against you:
Your twin losing the battle
Early in the process
While you persevered

You, my determined child,
Have set lofty goals for yourself
Seemingly from the very beginning
Higher goals than I could have imagined,
Unwilling to compromise to reach them
No matter what life threw in your way

You, my introspective child,
Must find this a bittersweet day -
Filled with the joy of accomplishment
Basking in the warmth of your loved ones
Even as you feel the loss of those present before
But passing on since your last graduation

You, my compassionate child,
Assisting others along your way
Often torn between your desire to be home
At times when family and friends were hurting
And your need to remain in school
To meet your degree requirements

You, my ADHD child,
Sometimes so full of energy, life and focus
That it is tough for the rest of us to keep up
While scattered and off the wall at others
Driving yourself into a tizzy
When reigning yourself in seems impossible

You, my honored child,
As you accept your masters in teaching
Must be filled with both joy and apprehension
As you wonder when your career will begin,
Consider just where it may lead
And how your life might change as a result

You, my engaged child,
Standing at the threshold of a union
Designed to provide love and support
Even as you provide the same to your chosen
In the home the two of you will establish
When you begin your journey as one

You, my grown-up child,
Your childhood now officially past,
Must now move into this complex world
Holding fast to your character and integrity,
Maintaining your belief and your faith
While others do their best to steal them

You, my precious child,
My beautiful and loving daughter,
Well-prepared to change the world
One student, one friend, one colleague,
One encounter at a time -
Go forth and light the world

I love you, Cindy,
You, my child, my only child

jbh: 5-7-05

<u>Just A Ring</u>

"Is there a particular reason you didn't take that piece of jewelry off before you came in for surgery?" the nurse asked the middle-aged woman as she was taking pre-operative "vitals".

"You mean other than I couldn't get it off before leaving home?"

"That's as good a reason as any I've heard since transferring to ambulatory surgery, I suppose. Do you mind if we try some of the tricks we've learned over the years?"

"That'd be great. When they slit my throat during last year's surgery, they just placed a piece of tape over the jewelry so it wouldn't distract the doc while he was operating. He said it was special tape that would make lots of noise in case someone tried to sneak it off my hand while I was in the operating room."

"Good Lord, woman, slit your throat! What kind of surgery were you having, anyway?"

"He was looking for a parathyroid tumor so he had to slice my throat to go hunting for it. I told him I couldn't be worried about anyone slipping a ring off my hand while a knife-wielding man was going to be moving my vocal chords and jugular vein around while looking for a little ole tumor. I had faith people on that staff could tell me where the best pawn shops were in Richmond. Once the doc did his job, my husband and daughter could hunt down the ring as my man has one just like it on his left ring finger. You just got to know who and what to trust, ya' know?"

The nurse went out of the cubicle, bent double in laughter, to go looking for a bed pan (for her) and lotion, string, and petroleum jelly for the patient. Three nurses, one anesthesiologist's assistant, and one orthopedic surgeon later, the quintessential issue arose: "Is this ring a matter of sentiment or a matter of it just won't budge for you, or anybody else?"

Jokingly, the patient said, "It's a matter of it won't come off for me and a matter of sentiment for my spouse."

Unflinchingly the surgeon replied, "Get the husband in here. He gets one shot at salvaging the ring. Then it goes."

"What mess have you stirred up now," the husband cracked as he entered his wife's cubicle. She held up her left hand which already showed the effects of having been in an iced glove for fifteen minutes, then squeezed every which way but off, and what seemed to be silver versus brass knuckles on her ring finger.

Reaching gently for her hand, he kissed her finger and said, "Let me give it a try." When it didn't budge, he just looked at his wife with sad eyes and said, "They're going to have to cut it off."

"The ring?" she asked.

"Yes," said the surgeon, nurse, and husband in unison.

"I just wanted to make sure I was going to get to keep the finger after all this." She was a little concerned the only one who didn't laugh was the surgeon.

When the bolt cutters were brought into the cubicle, she smiled bravely and told herself it was only a ring. Yes, a circular piece of white gold that could easily be replaced. She held her left hand out and prayed that it would be over soon so she could get on with the surgery she was scheduled to have that morning.

♥♥♥♥♥♥♥♥♥♥♥♥♥♥♥♥♥♥♥♥♥♥

I was not prepared for the flood of memories that rushed through my mind when I heard the first snip of the cutters. "Will you, Janice, take this man, Aubrey, to be your wedded husband, to have and to hold from this day forward..."

Small wonder that wedding band wouldn't come off my finger after 35 years, 2 months, and 30 days; 1 birthed child; thousands of school children; and God only knows how many jammed fingers from playing ball for over 30 years. Okay, okay, and those extra pounds put on during that time also made a difference.

Another snip of that cutter brought tears as I remember awakening from major surgery late one January night, in 1981, with Aubrey anxiously waiting to give me news from the ob/gyn: "Jan, we're going to have a baby." To this day, I'm embarrassed by my response to him. I went in for a D&C, a procedure that would have ensured there would be no baby if the doctor followed the set routine plus I had a huge surgical bandage that seemingly indicated I had a complete hysterectomy. I did not find his comment a bit amusing. As it turns out, the gynecologist changed course at the very last minute and cut over Cindy and took a pregnancy test directly from the womb. I find myself apologizing to Aubrey every now and then when I'm speaking publicly just to try to make up for that night.

Another snip. "Jan, she's beautiful and she looks like you."

It feels as if they're pulling my finger off. "Aubrey, I'm sorry. They need us to go back to the hospital. Your dad's not going to make it."

I think we're going to have to get a scalpel to cut this last little bit of ring off. "Who gives this woman to this man?"

"Her mother and I do."

Finally, the ring is off. I look at the once perfect circle of white gold that is now mangled but not beyond repair. With tears in my eyes, I hand it to Aubrey and ask him to keep it in a safe place until my left hand heals properly. I will have this ring remade but I will ask that it have several "scars" in it as reminders of time already spent together and for whatever time remains for us.

God provides us lessons in every situation if we are but willing to be still and listen to His voice as He speaks to us in so many different ways. Since November 4th, the day of my carpal tunnel and trapezium repair surgery, He has spoken to me in a variety of ways about my marriage. Our vows to each other were made before God in His sanctuary and before men. As long as Aubrey and I remember to keep God in our marriage, we will be fine. As with most married couples, there've been plenty of times I've wanted to take off my wedding rings and throw them as far as I could, preferably over a mountain range or while out at sea, but those vows are sacred, even now.

Just a ring? No, it is a symbol of a sacred vow that is at the root of my faith. This ring, ultimately, is replaceable; however, "what God has joined, let no man put asunder."

jbh
November 16, 2008

This story won First Place in Fanstory.com's Faith Non-Fiction Contest in November, 2008.

IT'S TIME TO GO

When you were young
You'd visit friends
Tarrying longer than you should
Testing your mother's patience
Until she firmly said,
"It's time to go!"

How different it became
When that school bell rang
Signifying the end of day –
Shoving your books into that desk
You were off and running
Before the teacher could say,
"It's time to go."

Sitting at the bus station
Trying not to cry
Willing time to stand still
Wishing World War II would go away
For you simply could not bear to hear
Your husband choke out,
"It's time to go."

Standing by a loved one's bed
Knowing there's little time left
Searching for the right words,
Dead tired, not wanting to leave,
A nurse tugs gently on your sleeve,
Guides you to the door, and whispers,
"It's time to go."

Now in your dreams you find
A vision of a faceless man
Draped in a garment of white
Waiting patiently for you –
Do not be afraid, Lil,
He's from heaven, you know,
He's there to tell you,
"It's time to go."

jbh
3-3-06

Aubrey

Earlier, I was struggling to get myself together
Driving us both to distraction in the house;
Now, settling behind the wheel of my car
I happened to glance your way –
There you sat in your vehicle
Gazing at me with eyes of love,
That charming boyish grin proclaiming,
"Relax; it's going to be okay."

A wave of love washed over me
Though you couldn't see it;
I was struck by how often
I take for granted
Your calming influence
Your gentle, steady ways
Which make me slow down and
Regroup in spite of myself

You have loved me those days
When I couldn't love myself
Stood by my side and held me
When each of my parents took journeys
Through illness and death
Never once complaining
When I neglected you
To care for them
For days on end

For as long as I can remember
You've been part of my life
From second grade
Through thirty plus years of marriage
You have enhanced my joy and
Shared my fears;
While I don't always tell you
I will always love you.

    jbh: 3-12-06

Good-Bye

Eyes brimming with tears
As they leave your side
Each visitor releases you to God;
Your eyes burn brightly in return
A knowing smile on your face –
Your demeanor reassuring us
You've lived for this moment
To meet your Lord and Savior;
No fear in your eyes
Knowing the future was determined years ago
By a simple invitation to Jesus Christ
To dwell in you from that day forth
Ensuring that when you breathe your last
He'll say to our Heavenly Father,
"Oh, Father, this one's with me,
By my blood I've set her free,
My resurrection her soul did win
Please, Father, bid Lil come in."

jbh
6-8-07

Going Home

Is that a tear I see on your face?
You're torn because it's time for goodbye
God has sent Ernest to take you away
Join friends and family who've gone ahead
Sing glory and praises to the Lord Almighty
Who long ago prepared your new home.

Go, now, you don't have to remain,
We will rejoin you one day, I believe,
Resurrection peace provides that guarantee
God has chosen this moment for you
Until it's our time, our memories must serve
To keep your dry humor and wisdom in mind
There's so much about you that'll certainly be missed
Our friend, aunt, neighbor, patient, loved one, sis.

We love you, Lil.

jbh
6-10-07

Your Struggles

The struggles are many, I know
You try not to let any of them show
But even with all your grace
The strain still shows on your face;

The tears you've come to despise
Threaten to spill from your eyes
As frustration pulls you apart
Shooting arrows straight to your heart;

It's not easy to be where you are
But, honey, you've come way too far
To give up and let the enemy win
By returning to old habits again;

You must think I don't understand
What it's like to follow your plan
So much happening and way too fast
With no way to know how long it will last;

You think I'm being critical when I'm not
Don't you know, Sunshine, you're all that I've got
I'll always be right here for you
My unconditional love is forever true;

No matter where all this may end
Count Jesus as Savior and friend
Give Him your struggles and tests
Then trust Him to take care of the rest.

jbh
7-15-07

Hearing My Granddaughter's Heartbeat

pure bonding moment
hearing daughter's child's heartbeat
snuggled in her womb

7-21-08

Three Generations

three generations
mother, daughter, granddaughter
love's purest circle

1-27-09

Snug

snug on my shoulder
sleeping soundly; music plays
bonding time for us

1-28-09

Great Expectations

rocking granddaughter
thinking about our future
great expectations

1-29-09
jbh

Friends

"God pairs people as friends at the right time and place and season of need."

--Wayne Watson

Friendship

I was looking for a friend, I needed one today.
　It was just a simple problem, one that
　　wouldn't go away.
This friend I needed is one to listen to my pain.
　　　And just to have her listen and listen
　　　maybe again.
Two shoulders to carry a burden, and two
　　　　hearts to hear a cry;
　　　It makes the burden lighter when my friend
　　　　is so close by.
Four hands to push or pull the load helps pass
　　　　the time of day;
Even on the longest night, right by me she
　　　　will stay.
At times we shared our laughter, and at times
　　　　we shared our tears.
So the friendship lasted, and will for many
　　　　years.
I had a friend as a little girl and then again as
　　　　a teen.
Everywhere along the way there was that
　　　　friend again.
A friend to share the happy times and a friend
　　　　to share the tears.
A friend for any weather, one that will
　　　　last for years.
I've said it before and I'll say it again,
You were here when I needed you,
Thanks for being my friend.

　　　Jeanne Banks
　　　October, 2007

Coincidences or Connections?

Like genies magically appearing
From treasured bottles
    letters
        phone calls
           emails
              visits
The magnetic field of camaraderie
Compelling contact for reasons unknown;
Telepathic connections by kindred hearts
Needing to share a myriad of emotions.

Some claim coincidence,
    intervention from others,
        imagination,
Tragic, life devoid of the joy
Of angels on earth called friends.

        jbh
        11-29-06

Friends and Family

Friends
All together
Loving, praying, laughing
Thinking no difference within
Family

Desirée Cote Bryant
January, 2008
6 years old

You Can't See My Pain

The pain has dulled
The shock worn away
Now there are only thoughts of dreams
That will never come true
And the realization
There was nothing, nothing
Either of us could have done
To prevent this tragedy.

I stare ahead but all I see is
The second you whispered, "Good-bye,"
Passing on to a better day
As I tenderly cradled your head
In my arms ~
Yet, somehow I know
I must find the strength to go on.

jbh
1974

Thank You, My Friend

I strive to find a simple way
To thank you from my heart
For you have done so much for me
I don't know where to start

How can I ever let you know
Exactly how I feel
For helping me get through times
That often seemed unreal

For always letting me feel free
To call you night and day
To share those things I felt I must
To help me find my way

For all those times you let me talk
So I could let off steam
You made me see that things were not
As bad as they had seemed

For sharing things both good and bad
In both your life and mine
I know that I've been mighty blessed
To have a friend so fine

You have the knack of knowing
Exactly how I feel
And do the little special things
That make a friendship real

For I know in all my years
Whether they be many or few
I'll never find another friend
As wonderful as you

       jbh
       1974

<u>For My Friend, Cindy</u>

If I only knew the words to use
To soothe your frustrations,
I'd say them –
But, somehow, between friends,
Words don't need to be shared
Because one already knows
How the other feels.

Just remain the great person you are
And believe all will work out for the best:
Be confident;
Be gracious;
Be loving and understanding;
And, above all,
Remember your friends when you need them
Because that's why you have us.

Take care of yourself, ok?

jbh
4-2-79

Please Look For Me Tomorrow

Please look for me tomorrow; I'll still be here with you
  You will see me if you try, in the little things you do.

Please look for me tomorrow, in the twinkle of an eye,
  Or the smiles of a stranger, as you go walking by.

Please look for me tomorrow, and laugh at the silly things
  I've done
  And don't forget to remember that we had a lot of fun.

Please look for me tomorrow when you hear my favorite
  song
  And if you know the tune just hum or sing along.

Please look for me tomorrow in the garden by the road
  In the singing of the song bird, it will surely ease the load

Please look for me tomorrow when I'm with those who've
  gone before
  I promise I'll be waiting for you on that beautiful shore.

Please look for me tomorrow and when you shed a tear,
  You are wrapped in arms of tender love by all the
    family there.

You will see me in the sunset or again at the dawn.
  And if you can't see me, it doesn't mean I'm really gone.

Please look for me tomorrow even if I'm gone from here,
  The gift from God of memory will keep me always near.

PLEASE, LOOK FOR ME TOMORROW!

    Jeanne Banks
    January, '08

Brittany Lester

Brightly smiling
Resolving to move back
Into
The world she knew before
Transverse myelitis,
A rare disease which
Nearly killed her;
Yet she

Loves life and appreciates
Every
Small step
Transporting her towards
Emotional and physical
Recovery

jbh
2007

EMILY, MY GIFT FROM GOD

Ever since I accepted you really do plan to retire
    in June
I have been trying to determine just the right words
    that could
In some small way make you understand just what a
    positive influence
You have been in my life over the last five and a half
    years

As I've told you before, I wasn't looking for either a
    friend or a lunch buddy
When I returned from my lengthy rehabilitation
    after knee surgery –
I was just being friendly and wanted to see for myself
The newest member of our administrative team

Who could've known we were destined to spend
    hours upon hours
Struggling with the angst that came with the early
    days of Even Start
Or how we would work together with guidance
    counselors in an attempt
To teach them CTE is definitely not our parents'
    vocational program?

From the first ride to the Print Shop to visit Benny
    (with chocolates, of course)
To teach you how to get on his good side
It became obvious the two of us had a great deal in
    common

We must have been the best of friends in a different
　　　　life as
We have laughed, cried, talked, walked, shared,
　　　　cared, played and worked together
As colleagues, best friends, proofreaders,
　　　　encouragers, builders of programs
All the time willing to tell each other what we were
　　　　thinking even when we knew
We would not necessarily see eye to eye

You have enriched my life in ways too numerous to
　　　　count
Ever so gently but firmly guiding me towards
　　　　becoming a better me
Especially during those dark times when I
　　　　became so lost
I barely even knew there was a me still in existence.

There are so many gifts you shared with me along the
　　　　way
Which have made such a difference in my life:
Faith, therapy, Sleep Comfort, friends, women's
　　　　ministry, music
But the most important of all is simply you

So many times we have discussed over a meal
There are no true coincidences in life
Rather there are carefully orchestrated intertwining
　　　　paths
Onto which God places us at different times

I believe God allows us the freedom to choose
How we interact with those we meet on those paths
Yet somehow the magnetism between some is so
    strong
The connection is almost a foregone conclusion

I will always be eternally grateful
God chose to intertwine our lives in such a way
Our friendship transcended both time and distance
I know I am a far better person because of your
    influence in my life.
Emily, truly, you are a gift from God.

       jbh
      06-2004

Losing Friends

I tell you repeatedly
I can't lose any more friends
Yet, the sad truth is
I suppose I can;
Life is frail, at best,
Fate will dictate things we can't control
I can force myself to deal with that
Because I haven't a choice
But to lose friends
To things which are controllable
Is bitterly unacceptable;
I rail against that possibility
Whether the loss be physical,
Mental, or emotional;
Either way, the loss is huge,
An integral part of my heart dies
Each time a friend passes to the other side
So I simply ask this:
Do what you must to stay sane,
Do what you can to remain healthy,
And always, always remember
Just how special you are to me.

    jbh
    10-16-00

What Was It, My Friend?

What was it, my friend,
You were sensing
When you wrote
Early that Sunday morning
Every time I think she's doing better
The bottom falls out again
Little could we have known
Before the day was over
Those words would become prophetic
As your world exploded
With your daughter's suicide
Three days before her sixteenth birthday

It's beyond my ability to conceive
The depth of your heartache and confusion
As you struggle to understand not only how
This could happen after working
Two and a half years to help her heal
After that horrible automobile accident
So many hurdles mastered through
Untold hours of hard work, tears, perseverance ~
Hours that must now seem like such a waste
As you rail at the fates
Questioning why she didn't talk to you
Finding you tempted to curse God

Cursing God, however, doesn't change things
Nor is any of this His fault, as you already know
Through His grace, He allowed you to know
Your daughter changed her mind and wanted to live
Calling for assistance and fighting tooth and nail
To remain on earth with family and friends

For whatever reason, it wasn't to be –
Her earthly body now traded for a heavenly one
Never again to know pain or sorrow
Trust God to provide you with all your needs
Until it is time to be reunited with her

I am praying for you, my friend

jbh
12-9-05

Inherent Problem

There's an inherent problem
When scheduled sessions end –
Society says call you therapist,
My heart insists on friend.
It is a situation
I won't bother to defend,
The honesty between us
Won't allow me to pretend.
Other words could be used
To describe roles you've played –
Counselor, mentor, beacon
The many times you've prayed,
Teacher, doctor, comforter
What compassion you displayed.
In all those ways, you walked with me
As my brokenness did mend,
Society may call you therapist
My heart knows you as friend.

jbh
5-21-06

<u>Journey of Best Friends</u>

tears from within our souls we've shared
laughed so hard we've lost our air
at the same atrocities we've glared
in the silence sometimes stared
as we've journeyed as best friends

we've managed somehow to get along
even though one of us is headstrong
and knew the other was plain wrong
still it's evident to all we belong
together on this journey as best friends

there's a difference in our age
you've become more of a sage
when we're not on the same page
or when I want us to engage
on another journey as best friends

I can see you're getting tired
even though I'm often wired
after all, it's by you I'm inspired
to get our families totally mired
in this journey of best friends

if my voice cracks as I speak
please forgive me for being weak
as I valiantly try not to speak
about how that door will surely creak
at the end of our journey as best friends

jbh
2-16-09

My Friend of Friends

My friend of friends, I fear for you
As you disappear more and more
Into the abyss heartache brings—
"No mas, No mas" your spirit screams
As you prepare for another loss
Rather than continue this endless fight.
Blessed with a warm and generous nature
You're always giving more
Than you're willing to take
Even to the point of financial harm
While keeping family members afloat
As they do little for themselves.

I can't tell you how to make things better
I won't have to live with the consequences
Of decisions that have to be made;
Do not withdraw from the support
Of the many friends who are
Willing to take this journey with you,
Tell me I have better things to do, or
You aren't very good company these days;
These are decisions I can make myself—
Let me divide your pain by sharing it
Just as you have helped carry mine for years,
Please, please, let me be here for you now.

jbh
10-27-05

DEBBIE'S H-E-A-R-T

There are no dry eyes in the room
By the time you've shared your story
Each touched in his or her own way
Struck by your courage and faith
As you've turned personal tragedy
Into a crusade for assisting victims without voices
By removing sexual predators off our streets
As you campaign tirelessly to raise awareness
About how DNA can link seemingly unconnected
      cases
To the same person whose violations have escalated
From crimes against property to crimes against
      persons.

Having first seen your testimony from afar
Before knowing you personally
And now from by your side as friend
I remain just as moved as your audience
Yet with a new perspective they likely cannot see –
There's a cost each time you recount the horrific
      details of March 3, 1989 which would forever
      change the lives of your family and friends –
Who could have blamed you had you chosen to
      resume what you could reclaim of your former life
Once Norman's trial was over and he was sentenced
      to jail for the remainder of his life?

Instead a Congressional Act bears your name
Signed into law by President George W. Bush
On October 30, 2004 as part of the Justice for All Act
As well as honors too numerous to name
Yet you remain humbled by it all
Never meaning to call attention to yourself
Just wanting the violence against women to stop;
For women who have been violated to realize they do
   have a voice;
Hope truly does Exist After Rape Trauma;
nothing they did gave anyone the right to hurt
  them;
there are many fighting to help make them safe
    and secure!

Through it all, your faith in a merciful God
Has provided you the strength to go on
Even on the darkest days when hope was dim;
fears were at the most extreme;
doubts clouded all you did –
You kept falling on your knees
Imploring God to show you the way
To turn what Satan meant for evil
Into a good work showing God's glory
Not only in your life but for the good of others –
Thus evolved Debbie's H-E-A-R-T!

    jbh
    12-15-05

GET WELL, MY FRIEND

I've always bared my soul to you so
Finding you in the hospital
Without hearing it from you
Has thrown me;
A chance visit has made me realize
How far apart we've grown
As I became so preoccupied in my world
I failed to notice things
Falling apart in yours
I offer no excuses
For prior inattention and
Seeming self-serving actions –
Just know how essential it is
For you to overcome this illness
So I can make it up to you
I will never take you for granted again

> jbh
> 11-17-76

<u>My Inspirational Friend, Temple</u>

Never have I been more impressed
By the depth of your faith
Or the strength of your spirit
As I have been the last few months
While you have shared the struggles
Regarding your health with me—
Others who received your emails
May not sense the intensity of the battles
As you never complain ~
You simply state there may be some troubles,
Your energy level is low,
Things which alert me you're not as well
As I wish you could be

Ever since meeting you at Longwood
On the halls of that old French dorm
Where you roomed with a math major I knew
You have inspired me with your fiery spirit,
Thirst for knowledge,
Dedication to friends,
Interest in space exploration,
Intensity while fencing,
Refusal to accept things at face value,
Journey to become a lawyer,
Empathy for others,
Faith in the face of tremendous setbacks, and
Desire to keep God close and personal

My life has been so deeply enriched
By our thirty-five years of friendship
Linked by memories of days spent
As Longwood Ladies in Farmville, Virginia
Further enhanced by letters and emails
Exchanged over the years
You, living on the west coast,

Me, firmly entrenched on the east,
Our ties remaining strong
Especially over the past few years
As we've shared from the depths of our hearts
Our concerns for each other
As well as our faith in a benevolent God

Now, as I reflect on your most recent email
Where you discussed appreciation of my musings
And slipped in your upcoming entry into hospice care
I realize your spirit remains alive and well
Even as you take the necessary steps
To gather extra assistance to become stronger
So you can make the decision about more chemo—
I will continue to pray, as you asked me to before,
That you find God near, real and present every day;
No matter what prayers others may offer on your
        behalf—
God will come to you and will minister to you
As long as you give yourself over to Him

I love you, Temple, as does God, our Heavenly
        Father. Godspeed, my friend!

        jbh
        1-8-06

*Temple passed into eternity
on March 24, 2006 after a
courageous six-year battle
with cancer. This poem was
shared with her shortly after
it was written.

Indelible Mark

I turn
Walk quietly away
From the place I first met you
Knowing it will always remain a part of me
No matter where I go
Or whatever I do.
You made an indelible mark
Upon every aspect of my life ~
You changed it
Made it real
Alive
Complete
So that even if you leave me behind one day
To follow the wind
I will have more than I had
Before you entered my life ~
The capacity to love
And be loved.

                    jab
                 10-25-70

FGHS, Class of '69

In June '65,
They closed our schools,
Said we'd adjust
To their new rules,
Said we'd make friends
With those we'd fought,
Said we'd learn things
We didn't want taught.

Unlike today,
They didn't plan
Orientations or parties
To help us understand;
Didn't give us a voice
About much of anything
Didn't even get
To design our ring.

From Holland, Whaleyville
And Chuckatuck, too,
From black schools and white schools
The mighty Rangers grew;
Some came with many friends
Others with only a few
All had the opportunity
Many others to accrue.

We learned compromise
And how to respect
Different strategies and traditions
There was much to inspect;
We became stronger together
Our horizons expanded
Never realizing at the time
Opportunities we'd been handed.

So, Forest Glen High School,
When from you we departed
It's safe, I'm sure, to say
Most were broken-hearted;
Leaving our precious school
With tears and looks behind,
But, so very proud to be called
The class of 1969.

jbh
9-30-06

Written in honor of my high school class and shared at our 35th class reunion!

Our Roller Coaster Ride

Although our professional association is ending
I cannot be sad
A journey like ours begins
With separation as its final goal
Neither knowing how long it will last
What will transpire along the way
Making each experience unique

Isn't it strange our journey become one
Challenging any of the world's top ten
Most thrilling, chilling rides
When neither of us likes roller coasters ~
Each professing great queasiness
At the thought of watching them
Dip, curve, and turn upside down

For over three years, we've traversed
Through illnesses, deaths, falls, broken bones,
Graduations, honors, lost jobs, new homes,
Retirements, and surprises too horrific to name
Always relying on God to provide
Insights, beacons, prayers, and processes
Leading to the peace and healing
I was so desperately seeking when I first called you

You had faith I would one day leave the nest
Gently but firmly requiring me
To test my wings each session
So when this time came
I would have the skills necessary
To deal with an unkind world

As our roller coaster glides to a stop
There will be new rules to follow
For this new journey on which I am about to embark
As I do what God has called me to
Not because I am already equipped
But because, through you, His messenger,
He has taught me to assist others as you have assisted
       me

From the first night you assured me
The only way to overcome fear was to face it head on
Perhaps we've both conquered our fear of roller
       coasters
By voicing that fear
Denying it power
Riding along with someone we trust
With complete faith in the One who holds us safe.

                    jbh
                    12-14-05

Former Student

Former student
Once the motivated
Now challenging me
In the pursuit of goals
Beyond my wildest dreams

Two people
Seemingly different
Yet forever bound
By family histories
Spanning almost fifty years

Long separated
Now reunited
As kindred spirits
Led by God's own light
Much to both our delight

Former student
Highly respected
Man of character
Believer in dreams
My friend, Nathan

jbh
8-20-06

In Memoriam

Tears mix with smiles
As we fondly remember
Those whose earthly journeys are ended;
Giving praise for lives touched
In special ways,
      Instruction rendered,
            Friendship extended,
Their lives forever intertwined
With each person they met -
Especially those they taught -
By the silver and gold threads of their
      Compassion
        Discipline
          Friendship
            Knowledge
              Laughter
         Love
       Strength
     Warmth
   Wisdom;
And those of us who love the red rose,
     Gold key
       And children still
Will interweave their threads
With new threads of our own
To pass to a new generation of students
Until we, like these we immortalize today,
Must also pass on.

        jbh
        4-29-07

Almeda

Never has love been more evident
Than in your tender touch
Your moist, gentle eyes
Both beg Glenn to remain
And grant him permission to ease into heaven

Discussions of your well-being are unnecessary
Reassurances to visitors all is well,
God has and will continue to provide;
A sense of peace pervades the room
Giving credence to your faith

Even in the darkest hour
Your concern is for others
Friends, family and the pastor
Must all get proper rest
As their plates are full

Almeda, quintessential caretaker,
Humbly assisting others whenever opportunities
        arise
Rarely asking anything in return
Questioning why anyone would help you
In this, your time of need

I am so honored
To be entrusted with Glenn's care
For these few hours
While you make preparations
For the celebration of his life

Wedding vows spoken from the heart
Promising to love and honor
To death do you part
Vows only partially true
You'll love him until you pass on, too

jbh
3-11-06

HESED 4 U

He said for you to listen carefully
From that spot in your rocking chair
To words not always spoken
From those His beacon led there;
He said their spirits are broken
By the evils of this world
Much of what they'll tell you
Will make those eyebrows curl;
He said take particular notice
When some clients tend to lie
Especially when they're adamant
Nothing can make them cry.
He said some might even teach you
Strategies you may not know
Things that will assist with others
Or even help you grow.
He said your exceptional insights
Are used with grace and care
He loves the way you give yourself
When personal experiences you share.
He said you don't have a clue
How much good you've done
How many lives forever changed
How many battles won.
He said He opened that school for you
To fulfill your destiny
Of nurturing people like your dad
Without having blood to see.

He said for you to take more time
To smell flowers every day
He loves that you always find time
In sessions, with clients, to pray.
He said for you to have no fear
When it's time for eternity
As Jesus will be there to welcome you
Saying, "Father, Martha's here with me."

jbh
9-19-07

My Best Friend

Can't imagine life without her
Angel sent here straight from God
Rarely does she make demands
Or fail to give her all
Lovingly, she stands by me
Yet kneels when I must cry
Never laughing when I fall

Could I find a better friend
Another person who
Really understands me
On days I barely do?
Lets me know I am important
Yes, it's my heart she truly sees
Nonetheless, she still loves me!

> jbh
> 1-27-08

When It's Time

When it's time for you to leave
Forgive me as I weep
Part of me you'll take along
Part of you I'll keep

I may be asked to share some words
Before we let you go
Some stories about the days before
Only you and I could know

Wouldn't they be shocked to hear
About those men in the hotel suite
In the little town of Troutville
Our faces red as beets

They missed the fun at Hallmark
As we laughed until we cried
The puddles we left on the floor
Couldn't be denied

Then there were those other times
We rode over to the Dairy Queen
Not so much for a chocolate fix
But to fix that which was unseen

Weekends spent below the state line
In trailers set side by side
Where we used to share so much
And sometimes just went to hide

Shopping trips could be a blast
We often didn't spend a dime
Because our real objective
Was to share some quality time

There were times we sat together
Waiting for surgeons to come and share
The outlook for family members
Who were going to be in their care

Those times when life got hectic
Keeping us too far apart
But never was there a single day
Without our best friend in our heart

One day someone will come to say
It's time for our last good-bye
No matter which of us goes first
We'll be rejoined one day on high

But should you go before I do
Forgive me as I weep
The best of me you'll take along
The best of you I'll keep

> jbh
> 6-24-09

ABOUT THE ARTIST & PHOTOGRAPHER

Craig Lowell is a native of Suffolk, Virginia. He began creating artwork in 1981 when he was only six years old. When given a large box of crayons, he was quickly inspired by the endless possibilities he could create. From the beginning, family members were impressed with both his technique and his ability to translate an idea into a beautiful picture. Craig specializes in landscapes and pen and ink drawings of historical buildings. His desire is for future generations to use his work as representations of the world as it was for their ancestors.

This is Craig's second book cover. His artwork is also showcased on the cover of <u>Beacons, Prayers, and Processes: Pathways to Healing</u> by Janice B. Holland. Limited edition digital copies of both paintings used for the covers are available by contacting the author. Contact Craig for either artwork or design work at cclowell01@gmail.com.

Eric P. Brooks was a native of Fayetteville, N.C., moving to Suffolk, Virginia in 1961. He began his photography career in 1962 at the Suffolk Raceway and The Virginian-Pilot while also free-lancing for the Suffolk News-Herald and the Daily Press. Eric was affectionately known as "Flash", for 40 years he shot Class Winning photos for the U.S. Nationals at Indianapolis, Indiana. He was also the track photographer for Langley Speedway. Eric taught photography at Tidewater Community College and Paul D. Camp Community College. Eric won many awards for his photos. Eric began photographing from heaven on June 17, 2009 and is sorely missed by all who knew him.

ABOUT THE AUTHORS

Janice Brown Holland is a retired educator and a native of Suffolk, Virginia. When writing this book, she asked several of her friends as well as her daughter, Cindy, to allow her to use some of their works to make this a true "faith, family, and friends" project.

The youngest contributor is Desirée Bryant. As a toddler, she would visit Janice's terminally ill mom some Sundays after church which brightened her mom's day greatly. Desirée is very special to the Holland family.

Jeanne Banks is a longtime friend and confidante. She writes poems for special occasions—especially for Pilot Club and Relay for Life events. She is especially known for her special brand of friendship and her beautiful singing voice. Jeanne has extraordinary energy and is the consummate volunteer.

Marcia Gray became Janice's "little sister" during the 1980-1981 school year which was her first year of teaching and, ironically, Janice's last year as she became an administrator the next year. Marcia is well known for her wonderful Christmas poems which were used as her school's Christmas cards for many years.

Cindy Holland Devers is a fifth grade teacher who began her teaching career one week after her mom, Janice, retired as assistant superintendent. The only child of Janice and Aubrey Holland, Cindy is married to David Devers II. Cindy and David are the proud parents of a daughter, Lexi, who was born in January, 2009.

Janice extends a special thanks to each of the contributors to this collection of poems and stories. She would also like to thank everyone who has read any of her works.

Ordering Books

Autographed copies of this book and/or Janice's first book, <u>Beacons, Prayers and Processes: Pathways to Healing</u>, may be ordered by contacting Janice at Rdfrdmom2@aol.com.

Upcoming Books

A selection of Janice's spiritual poetry is included in <u>Tapestry: Poetic Threads of Life</u> which became available Christmas, 2010.

Look for Janice's third book, <u>Cries in the Dark</u>, a handbook outlining additional things she feels are important for Hotline volunteers to know prior to being assigned a block of volunteer time. Autobiographical in nature, this book should be completed by the end of 2011.

Janice is also writing a book for her granddaughter entitled <u>Dear Lexi</u>. Volume I should be completed in 2011.

At her daughter Cindy's suggestion, Janice is also putting together a book to be entitled <u>Acrostically YOURS</u>, a set of acrostic poems to honor God. It should be out by Christmas, 2011.

Janice's dear friend, Temple Harvey, suggested she pen a book entitled <u>Musings</u> in which she would include any writings which did not necessarily fit a particular category. This is being compiled in Temple's memory and will be dedicated to her. There is no anticipated completion date for this book.